A COMPREHENSIVE LOOK AT THE OTHER RAILWAYS OF LONG ISLAND
PART ONE

THE
SHORTLINE RAILROADS OF LONG ISLAND
A COMPENDIUM

by

Harold Fagerberg
and
Edward M. Koehler Jr.

Brooklyn Dock & Terminal Railway
Brooklyn Eastern District Terminal
Bush Terminal Railroad
Degnon Terminal Railroad
Jay Street Connecting Railroad
New York Dock Railway
South Brooklyn Railway
The Trunk Line Railroad Terminals in Brooklyn

Maps prepared by George Wybenga

ISBN Number 978-0-9886916-1-2
This book copyright 2013 by the Long Island Sunrise Trail Chapter,
National Railway Historical Society.
Narrative copyright 2013 by Edward M. Koehler Jr.

**Published by the
Long Island Sunrise Trail Chapter
National Railway Historical Society
Post Office Box 507
Babylon, New York, 11702-0507
Printed in the United States of America**

Book Committee: Michael Boland, Eugene Collora, and Kenneth Katta.

Stephen F. Quigley	President
Robert L. Myers	Vice President
Craig Ash	Secretary
Alan Mark	Treasurer
Benjamin T. Young Jr.	National Director

INDEX

Dedications	v
Preface	vii
The Brooklyn Terminals	1
A New York Central System View from 1921	
The Williamsburg Connection	9
Brooklyn Eastern District Terminal (East River Dock and Terminal)	
The Immortal Shortline of Dieseldom	21
Jay Street Connecting Railroad	
Hoods Units, Boxcars, and Buildings	29
Bush Terminal Railroad	
Appendix I – Brooklyn Rapid Transit Cars leased to the Bush Terminal	40
Appendix II – The Industrial Railways of the Bush Terminal Area	41
Down on the Brooklyn Docks	45
New York Dock Railway (Brooklyn Wharf and Warehouse)	
The New York Dock Railway at Bush Terminal	51
Miss Phoebe Snow of Brooklyn, New York	59
Brooklyn Dock and Terminal Railway	
Delaware, Lackawanna and Western Railroad	
Mainland Mainline – Island Shortline	67
Baltimore and Ohio Railroad – Central Railroad of New Jersey	
Erie Railroad – Lehigh Valley Railroad – New York Central System	
New York, New Haven and Hartford Railroad – Pennsylvania Railroad	
A Queens Mystery?	75
Degnon Terminal Railroad	
The Last Street Railway in Kings County	81
South Brooklyn Railway	
A First Class Interurban on the South Brooklyn Railway	101
Finis	
Epilogue	107
Bibliography	109

- * * * -

The pictures on the cover are clockwise from the top left Brooklyn Eastern District Terminal 7; Jay Street Connecting Railroad 5; Bush Terminal Railroad second number 5; South Brooklyn Railway (New York Transit Authority period) 9980; Pennsylvania Railroad 3906; and New York Dock Railway 34. Further details and credits for these photographs can be found in the chapters on each of their lines.

- * * * -

DEDICATIONS

The Long Island Sunrise Trail Chapter, National Railway Historical Society proudly dedicates this volume to the late Harold Fagerberg (January 8, 1914 to October 29, 2009) who dearly loved and preserved the railway history of the Long Island region.

Harold's father was a carpenter on the Long Island Railroad who helped build the wooden runway for 'Mile-a-Minute' Murphy back in 1899. Harold worked for Roulston's Grocery Chain in the 1930's. Harold was taking railroad photographs as far back as the early 1930's. Harold was friendly with other rail photographers of the era including Charles Chaney, Joe Lavelle, Harold Goldsmith, Bill Bissinger, etc. Harold wanted to work for the Long Island Rail Road but no jobs were available. Probably about 1939 a friend (possibly G.W. O'Connor) who worked for the New York, New Haven and Hartford Railroad told Harold they were hiring and he got a job with them. Harold originally lived in Richmond Hill and made many excursions to Morris Park to photograph Long Island Rail Road motive power, he would sometimes go on a daily basis as the dates on his photographs suggest.

Harold lived in Hollis along side the Long Island Rail Road mainline for many years before moving to Babylon. He was a veritable fount of information on the Long Island Rail Road. Harold also photographed many of the other New York City area railroads and traded photographs with other railfans as was common in this era. As a result a few of the Charles Chaney Photographs in the Smithsonian Institution were actually taken by Harold!

Back in the 1930's Harold roamed Long Island in his first car, he told many that this vehicle had cost him the then princely sum of $20.00! Besides Morris Park, some of his favorite spots for photographing the Long Island Rail Road were Floral Park, New Hyde Park, Ronkonkoma, Jamaica and Montauk. He had a special interest in the mainline through Queens County.

When Harold passed on October 29, 2009 it created a hole in the fabric of New York Metropolitan area railroad history. The Long Island Sunrise Trail Chapter is gratified that Harold's family has seen fit to pass on to it Harold's collection of photographs from the Brooklyn dockside railroads.

Ronald Zinn
January 2013
On behalf of the
Long Island Sunrise Trail Chapter
National Railway Historical Society

- * * * -

Author Edward M. Koehler Jr. would like to dedicate this book to his late father who took him as a small child on automobile trips to explore the trolleys, electric buses, and other sites on the Brooklyn and Queens waterfronts. Many hours were spent watching the Long Island Rail Road unload carfloats in Long Island City. Ed would also like to dedicate this work to his wife Melissa who has suffered through the creation of this work along with his various other sundry pursuits. And finally Ed must also dedicate this work to the memory of his late son Mark,

Edward M. Koehler Jr.
Bayside, New York
January 2013

- * * * -

ONE FINAL DEDICATION

For over a century and a half the dedicated employees of the various railways that once populated the Queens and Brooklyn waterfront daily went about their jobs. Regardless of whether their title was engineer, fireman, conductor, brakeman, motorman, clerk, yardmaster, tugboat captain, deckhand, barge hand, maintenance of way worker, manager, or even owner; they were all responsible for the history that you are about to read.

On May 13, 1959 Gene Collora visited the Pigeon Street yard of the Brooklyn Eastern District Terminal and captured these fine images of a steam locomotive engineer performing his timeless duties.

It is to all of these individuals and the rich heritage that they have collectively created and continue to create for us to study and enjoy, that this volume is also respectfully dedicated.

PREFACE

A grammar school geography book given to this author in the fourth grade stated that the only railway on Long Island was the aptly named Long Island Railroad (sic). Knowledgeable students of the subject (and this included myself in the fourth grade) can quickly point to other companies such as the then Pennsylvania Railroad, the Brooklyn Eastern District Terminal, or more recently Amtrak, as railroads having a presence on Long Island. Needless to say my teacher back in grammar school was not impressed with either my knowledge or the constructive criticism that I was offering.

My interest in the little terminal railways down on the docks in Brooklyn (and a little bit in Queens) continued. Eventually, as a member of the Long Island Sunrise Trail Chapter of the National Railway Historical Society I came into contact with the late Harold Fagerberg who was a treasure trove of information on these interesting little railroads. Without Harold I am afraid that this material would be sorely lacking in substance.

The pictures in this book are typical of what a 1930-1940's railfan would have had. The enthusiast of that day would visit a yard or engine facility and attempt to secure multiple front three quarter images of each locomotive there, hopefully with the rods down. Our erstwhile buff would then trade the extra negatives with others of a similar interest so each could build up their own collection. As camera technology became better and film prices dropped after World War II the 'railroad action shot' that many of us are more familiar with became the staple of the rail buff's photo collection.

All of the images in this publication, unless otherwise credited are from the collection of Harold Fagerberg; they were donated to the Long Island Sunrise Trail Chapter of the National Railway Historical Society by Harold's family.

I would like to thank Gene Collora, Robert Delmonico, Jeff Erlitz, Phillip Goldstein, the late Richard Harrison (via Robert Myers), Dick Horn, Kenneth Katta, John Scala, Benjamin W. Schaeffer, Steven Rappaport and Joseph Torregrose for their photographic contributions to this project. Without these additional images this work would be sorely lacking in many areas. Not all of the contributed images were used, but then not all of the images from the collection of Harold Fagerberg were used in this publication. Thanks are also due to Michael Boland for providing the 1958 **Long Island Railroader** article on the Degnon Terminal and to the late F. Rodney Dirkes for giving the author access to the 1921 New York Central System article on the New York Harbor terminals. Many thanks to Gene Collora for his hours of darkroom work with the material from the Fagerberg collection. This material would be sorely lacking without the artwork contributions of George Wybenga. I would also like to commend fire buff buddy Ira Rubin, Dispatcher 26 of the Jersey City Fire Department for some key information concerning the Warren Street facility of the Brooklyn Eastern District Terminal.

I could prattle on but a 1921 article that appeared in the employee's magazine of the New York Central System seems to be a much more efficient way to start this material.

Edward M. Koehler Jr.
April, 2013

THE BROOKLYN TERMINALS

A NEW YORK CENTRAL SYSTEM VIEW FROM 1921

C.L. Jellinghaus

Originally Titled

BROOKLYN TERMINAL ROADS FEED MUCH TRAFFIC TO THE NEW YORK CENTRAL

- * * -

THE BROOKLYN TERMINALS
A NEW YORK CENTRAL SYSTEM VIEW FROM 1921[1]
C.L. Jellinghaus

There is something romantic and impressive about New York Harbor. Yet it is of simple outline and its' component parts are easily pigeonholed. I remember some years ago taking a sight seeing trip through the waterways of Rotterdam; what a blurred picture of canals, inlets, basins, and quays was retained. A few strokes of the pencil will form the contour of New York Harbor while we placidly state that New York is the largest city in the world and has the largest volume of overseas traffic of any port in the world.

We would draw practically a straight line to indicate the Long Island waterfront as the eastern boundary of the port, and there plot the four Brooklyn terminals to cover nearly a quarter of the distance from Long Island City to Bay Ridge. In railroad parlance, these are the 'contract' terminals, common to all the harbor roads[2], serving them disinterestedly but only incidentally as agents. For it is a mistake to think (as a good many do) that those terminals perform purely a railroad service.

Their beginning was in local enterprises, in the warehousing and transshipments of ocean traffic, and in manufactories. The requirements of these commercial developments and the economical and prompt handling of the resultant traffic led step by step from the trucking of freight between the New York City stations and the terminals to the handling by lighter and finally to the floating of freight in cars. Gradually also the terminals undertook with their team track and freight house facilities to serve an extensive 'hinterland' of industrial life, as well as the needs of a large residential section.

Each of the terminals – Bush, New York Dock, Jay Street, and the Brooklyn Eastern District is a distinct unit and an 'island' from a railroad operating standpoint. The terminals handling the traffic on a contract basis to and from the railroad float bridges with their own marine equipment, tugs, and car floats. In the case of the New York Central System, all of this traffic is handled over either the Weehawken or Sixty-Eighth Street[3] float bridges, none of the terminals having an all rail connection with any of the harbor railroads except Bush, which can be reached through the Long Island Rail

---

[1] This article originally appeared in the January 1921 issue of the New York Central System's employee magazine, the **New York Central Lines**. The coverage then was as a news story; today it is a valuable historical snapshot. The changes to the original article include the title, it was originally "Brooklyn Terminal Roads Feed Much Traffic to the New York Central", the deletion of three images of boxcars located in rail yards and the addition of footnotes which was done in June 1986 when it was published in **The Semaphore**, the publication of the Long Island – Sunrise Trail Chapter of the National Railway Historical Society. Do note the lack of any mention of the Pennsylvania Railroad. Sharp eyed readers will also notice the lack of coverage of the Delaware, Lackawanna and Western Railroad facilities and the Wallabout Basin pier head stations.

[2] The harbor railroads at the time of this article were considered to be the Baltimore and Ohio Railroad, the Erie Railroad, the Central Railroad of New Jersey, the Lehigh Valley Railroad, the Pennsylvania Railroad, the Delaware, Lackawanna and Western Railroad, the New York Central, the New York, New Haven, and Hartford Railroad, the Long Island Rail Road, and the Central New England Railroad (via lighters from Fishkill Landing, New York!). The South Brooklyn, the New York, Susquehanna, and Western Railway, the Staten Island Rapid Transit, and the New York, Ontario, and Western Railway all utilized the facilities of other lines to handle their harbor traffic; the Harlem Transfer, while a subsidiary of the Delaware, Lackawanna, and Western Railroad, was considered a terminal railroad in its own right.

[3] This was located at the foot of West Sixty-Eighth Street and the Hudson River in the borough of Manhattan.

Road and the Army base; but this route is not generally used and there are no through rates in effect[4].

The terminals receive their remuneration for the service performed by them for the railroads as a terminal allowance, a fixed portion of the rail rate[5]. All freight moving over the New York Central System is billed either through the Weehawken or the Sixty-Eighth Street stations and waybills are taken into account at those points, the New York Central System preparing the freight bills and accompanying copies and delivering them to the terminals with the cars; and on the westbound freight, the terminals either furnish a waybill form with all the forwarding data except through charges, or the original shipping orders for each shipment. The railroad company, in either case, re-bills on the standard waybill form.

Brooklyn Eastern District Terminal

In 1854, Havermeyer, Townsend, and Company established, on the East River in the Williamsburg section of Brooklyn, at the foot of South Third Street, the first unit of what was to become one of the largest sugar refineries in the United States – the Havermeyer and Elder Refinery. During the early years the sugar traffic originating at this refinery was lightered by small sail lighters to the railroad terminals and this method of handling continued until 1876, when the Erie Railroad entered into a contract with Palmer's Dock (Lowell M. Palmer managing the property for the Havemeyer and Elder interests until 1906 when it was reorganized as the Brooklyn Eastern Terminal[6]) under which the terminal company undertook the present carfloat service with it's own equipment. Brooklyn Eastern District Terminal, therefore, may be said to have had its origins in a plant facility, and from the railroad standpoint was the forerunner of the Brooklyn Terminals as we know them today.

At that time, Williamsburg, now a part of the Borough of Brooklyn, was but a small village, and manufacturing plants were only beginning to be established. In order to meet the rapid commercial development in that section, the carfloat arrangement entered into with the Erie Railroad was followed by a similar agreement with the New York Central and West Shore railroads in 1884, and with the Lehigh Valley, Baltimore and Ohio, and the Central Railroad of New Jersey soon afterward, while the Delaware, Lackawanna and Western and the New England lines availed themselves of these facilities only after the reorganization of the terminal in 1906. In that year the terminal company took over and greatly enlarged the property previously operated under the name of Palmer's Dock. All of the stock is owned by the Havemeyer and Elder interests, who before the formation of the American Sugar Refining Company owned the refinery named after them and several other large sugar refineries in the same district.

The original terminal layout consisted of only about a half block of property on the East River between North Fourth and North Fifth Streets, while today the main terminal station extends from North Third to North Tenth Streets and runs back some three blocks from the river front to Berry Street and serves the entire district between Wallabout Basin and Newtown Creek, in which some twenty-five hundred to three thousand consignees are located.

The terminal is the center of the hay trade for all of this district, and has on its tracks a hay shed with a capacity of two hundred fifty cars, equipped with modern machinery for handling this

---

[4] During the World War I period when the United States Railroad Administration ("USRA") had control of common carrier lines, the New York Central System had trackage rights over the Hell Gate Bridge and the Long Island Rail Road's Bay Ridge branch to both the Bay Ridge float bridges and the Army base.
[5] This is an amount equal to the movement of the commodity being transported for a distance of seventy-five miles.
[6] The company traded as the East River Terminal Company prior to 1906.

THE SHORTLINE RAILROADS OF LONG ISLAND

BROOKLYN EASTERN DISTRICT TERMINAL (continued)

commodity. The shed also has accommodations for the storage of flour as well as merchandise. In the territory immediately contiguous and on the tracks of the terminal company are the plants of the Brooklyn Cooperage Company[7], manufacturers of sugar barrels; Austin Nichols and Company, one of the largest wholesale grocers in the United States; the Standard Oil Company of New York; and the Scranton and Lehigh Coal Company, one of the largest coal distributors in Brooklyn.

The terminal yard has a capacity of six hundred fifty cars, included in which is space for four hundred team track cars. The modern less than carload freight house has eighteen delivery and receiving doors, and a car placing capacity of twenty eastbound and twenty-three westbound cars. The marine equipment consists of four of the latest steel tugs, fourteen car floats, and ten locomotives to handle the traffic at this and the other stations of the terminal company, for in addition to the main property it maintains a station at the foot of Pigeon Street, Long Island City and a pier station in Queensborough, Long Island City.

Jay Street Terminal

Jay Street Terminal (sic), while comparatively small compared with the other Brooklyn terminals, handles a large and important part of the rail traffic moving through New York Harbor. It has its beginning in 1904 when it was organized to take care of the rail requirements of a number of important industries, notably Arbuckle Brothers, dealers in sugar and coffee[8].

Jay Street is located just north of the Brooklyn Bridge, not many blocks from the north end of the New York Dock property, and between the latter and the Brooklyn Eastern District. The larger proportion of its traffic is in connection with the Arbuckle Brothers, and also with the Robert Gair Company, paper; Kirkman and Son, soap; and Jones Brothers, tea; consisting of raw materials eastbound, and manufactured articles, import sugar and coffee westbound. In addition, the terminal has an adequate public freight house and team track facilities for a considerable volume of general freight traffic.

There are six piers, two of which are leased to the Caribbean Steamship Company, two used for the delivery of carload freight, and one assigned to coastwise steamship traffic. The yard has a working capacity of two hundred fifty cars, and a freight house with a capacity of twenty-five cars. One float bridge takes care of the rail interchange, together with three stream locomotives[9], and marine equipment of two tugs, two steam lighters, and one open lighter. Unlike the other terminals, Jay Street does a considerable business in connection with the coastwise and Long Island Sound lines and handles import freight from steamships berthed at other points in the harbor.

---

[7] The Brooklyn Cooperage Company operated a number of lumber hauling railroads in the forests of the Northeast but had no railway presence in Brooklyn.
[8] This company sold coffee under the "Martinson" brand name.
[9] In actuality, the Jay Street Connecting was operating only two steam locomotives at this time, the third piece of motive power was a double truck gasoline-electric locomotive, the second one to have been built by the General Electric Company.

Bush Terminal

Few of us who know the Grand Central Zone have failed to notice the beautiful thirty-one story "Bush Terminal Sales Building"[10] or the "International Exhibit Building" as it is sometimes called. But probably not many of us have thought of it as related to railroad service and traffic moving over the New York Central to and from Bush Terminal in Brooklyn.

The relation is simple enough. Where the Exhibit Building brings together manufacturer and merchant from all parts of the world by means of its permanent exhibit of manufactured goods, in other words, sells goods and creates markets, the Bush Terminal property in south Brooklyn near the entrance to the harbor provides facilities where these goods are manufactured, stored, and shipped.

Bush Terminal was founded by Irving T. Bush a quarter of a century ago when congestion at the piers and warehouses in lower Manhattan suggested development in south Brooklyn to secure better facilities for the distribution of freight traffic. Its growth was rapid, and a terminal railway today links into one unit fifteen modern loft buildings accommodating three hundred commercial enterprises manufacturing hundreds of different commodities; one hundred twenty-three warehouses; and eight steamship piers. The property covers approximately two hundred acres.

The factory buildings, six to eight stories in height, are of the most modern reinforced concrete design with a floor area of more than five million square feet. They are built in units of two, each pair occupying a city block, and are served by two tracks, placed between, at the stub end of which joint platforms are provided. The warehouses have twenty-six million cubic feet of space, each with direct rail connections. The piers vary in length from six hundred to one thousand three hundred fifty feet, and are leased to twenty-seven different steamship companies, the area of one double deck pier representing a floor space of fifteen acres.

The Bush Terminal Railway, with twenty-three miles of track, eight steam locomotives and four electric motors, a yard of a thousand car capacity, team tracks for one hundred cars, and a general less than carload freight house; supplies adequate service not only to the Bush facilities proper but to a number of private sidings not located within the Bush layout. A marine fleet of two tugs and ten carfloats is the connecting link with the harbor railroads.

Bush Terminal has connections with the South Brooklyn Railway, the Army Base, and the United States Navy Supply Depot, and handles some of the traffic for these facilities to and from the rail terminals. The rail connection with the Long Island Rail Road[11] at Bay Ridge is through the Army Base.

---

[10] This structure is located on the south side of West Forty-Second Street between the Avenue of the Americas and Broadway.

[11] At this time the Long Island Rail Road was a subsidiary of the Pennsylvania Railroad, the New York Central's arch rival.

New York Dock Company

Back in 1886 keen competition among the various warehouse companies on the Brooklyn waterfront between the Brooklyn Bridge and the Erie Basin led to their consolidation into the Brooklyn Wharf and Warehouse Company, and this term is still used in our (New York Central System) Weehawken Yard where cars are carded for the "B.W.W." in spite of the fact that in 1901 the company was reorganized as the New York Dock Company. It was originally a warehouse proposition for overseas traffic supported by piers leased to various steamship lines, which in later years was expanded to include a large number of manufacturing establishments, a less than carload freight station, and adequate team tracks for local deliveries.

This terminal is located a short distance north of the Bush Terminal, and roughly parallels the service performed by the latter. New York Dock has the most extensive waterfront of any private company in the harbor and, except for the city owned piers, the largest number of piers under one control leased to steamship companies.

There are three distinct units in the layout – Fulton, Baltic, and Atlantic terminals separated from each other by a few city blocks, but with no rail connection, so that floats moving to and from the railroad terminals are usually handled at Fulton Terminal, and cars refloated to the other two terminals as conditions require.

There are thirty-three piers, with a floor area of over two million square feet, and these are leased to fourteen different steamship lines, their steamships plying to all parts of the world. These piers vary in length from four hundred to over a thousand feet, and some have tracks running their entire length. There are forty-four manufacturing plants, and forty-seven private sidings served by a railway with 9.93 miles of track. The three units have team tracks with a total capacity of about one hundred fifty cars, the working capacity of the various yards being four hundred fifty cars. Team tracks are in regular use only at Baltic and Atlantic terminals and a less than carload freight station is located at the latter point. To handle its business, the New York Dock operates four locomotives, four floatbridges, and marine equipment consisting of two powerful tugs, eight floats, and four barges.

Among the more important firms with sidings on New York Dock property may be mentioned the National Cold Storage Company, Nestle's Food Company, the American Can Company (Dock Factory), Franklin-Baker Company, and the Great Atlantic and Pacific Tea Company.

- * * * -

Perhaps it is a quiet Sunday afternoon in 1959, but regardless of the day no less than four Delaware, Lackawanna and Western Railroad tugboats are tied up in Hoboken. Soon engines will be revved up, lines cast off and carfloats will begin to be moved, perhaps some to 25th Street in Brooklyn? This is a Norman Kohl image from the John Scala collection.

THE SHORTLINE RAILROADS OF LONG ISLAND

THE WILLIAMSBURG CONNECTION

BROOKLYN EASTERN DISTRICT TERMINAL

- * * * -

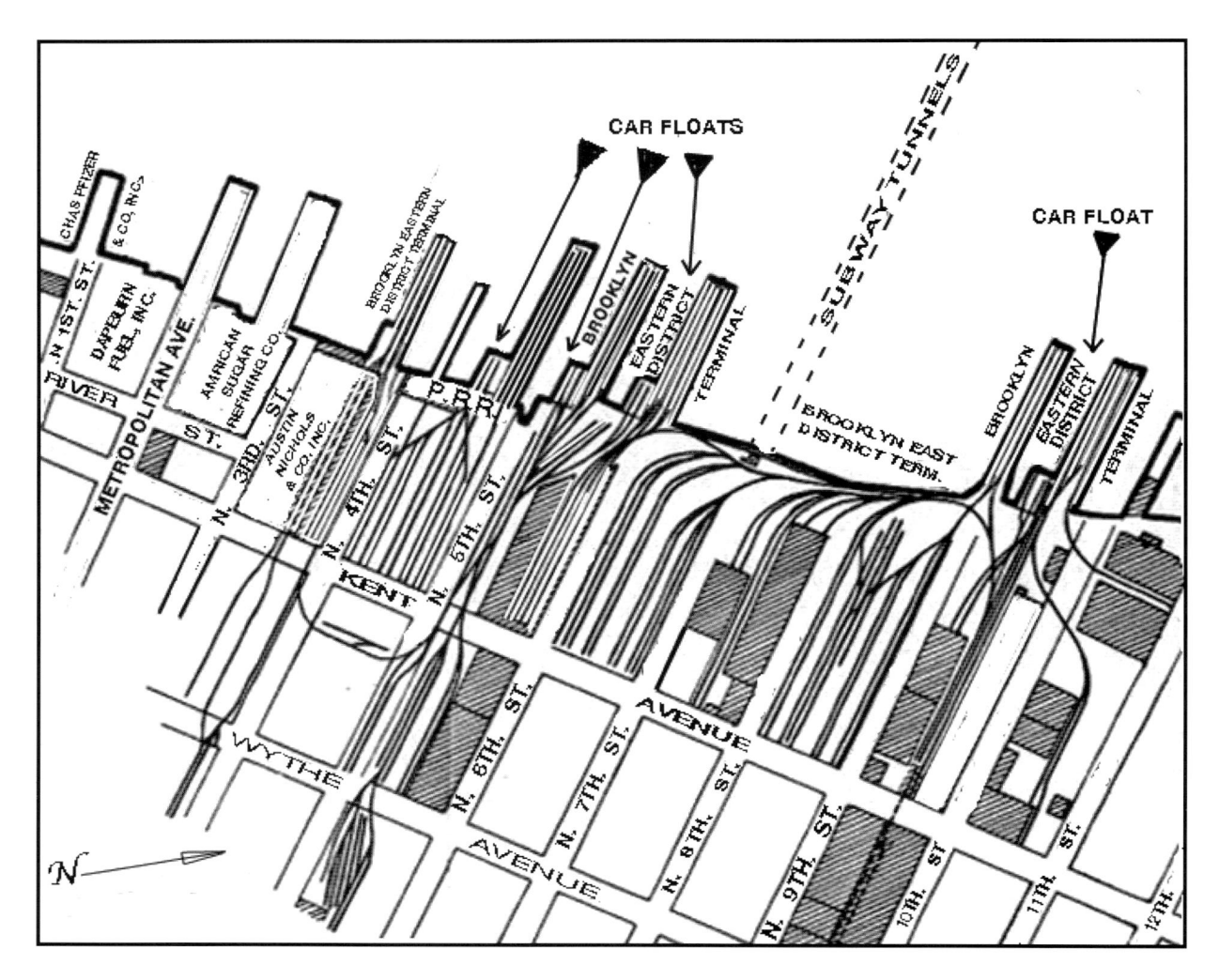

(Above) A United States Army Corps of Engineers map of the Brooklyn Eastern District Terminal's Kent Avenue complex as reworked by George Wybenga. Note the independent trackage in the block bounded by North 4th Street, Kent Avenue, and North 5th Street; this was the Pennsylvania Railroad's North 4th Street freighthouse. The symbol ▼ used on this and the other maps in this volume indicates a railroad carfloat. (Below) Another Corps of Engineers map of the Pigeon Street Terminal in Long Island City. Note that there was no physical connection between the BEDT and the Long Island Rail Road's Long Island City yard.

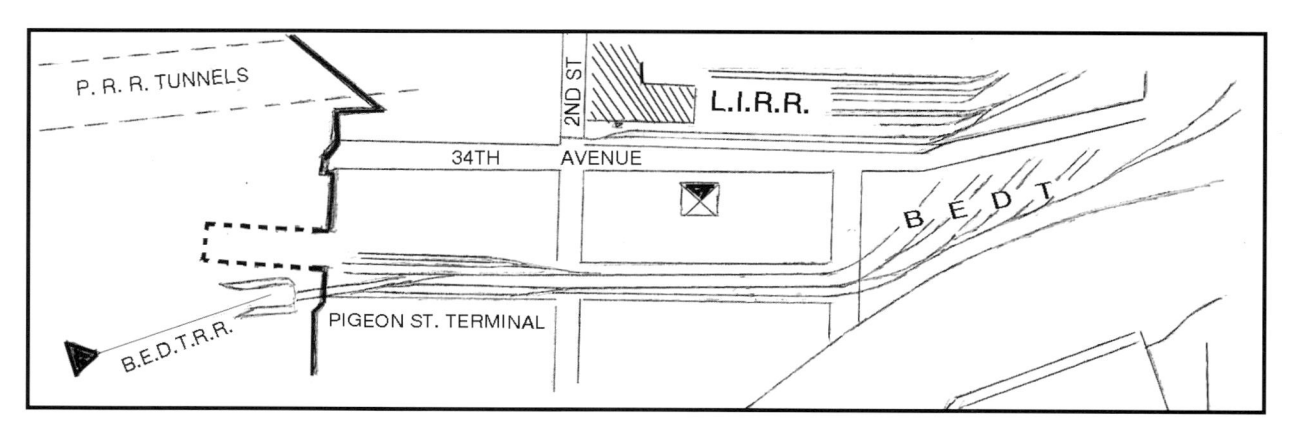

THE WILLIAMSBURG CONNECTION
The Brooklyn Eastern District Terminal

The earliest firm organized by the Havemeyer sugar interests during 1875 was the East River Terminal Company which took over the operations of the older Palmer Dock Company that dated to 1870 and served the 'Jack Frost' sugar refineries and their related facilities in Williamsburg. The operation was reincorporated in 1906 as the Brooklyn Eastern District Terminal and under the life of that name served several distinct terminal areas. The northern most portion of the road was located across the Queens County line in Astoria and was known as the Queensborough Pier Terminal at 13th Street in Long Island City; this facility opened in 1914 and closed circa 1930; there were no rails at this location, only a pier where lighters and carfloats could tie up and be serviced from the pier. The next southern facility in Long Island City was known as Pigeon Street and was opened in 1906. Despite its having been located just yards south of the Long Island Rail Road's passenger facility there, no physical connection ever existed. The Pigeon Street yard, in its heyday served a sugar refinery and after that closed; a distributor for Miller Beer. Corporate changes at the Miller Brewing Company not only took them out of Milwaukee, their traditional home; it meant an end to the fleet of insulated box cars delivering the suds to the various distributors throughout the country. As a result the yard was no longer used after 1976 and construction in the area gradually eradicated the site.

Brooklyn Eastern District Terminal 14 began life as the number 5 at the Mesta Machine Works in West Homestead, Pennsylvania. It is seen here on an unknown date in the Pigeon Street Terminal. Today this locomotive is on the Delaware and Ulster Railroad in upstate New York and is subject to a cosmetic restoration.

A short carfloat trip south down the East River is the main Eastern District portion of the railroad. Crossing North Kent Avenue from North Twelfth to North Third Streets and at South Third Street was the heart of the Brooklyn Eastern District Terminal. A large sugar refinery was also located here, but it was closed in the early sixties, reducing consignees here to a paper distributor and several scrap merchants. The road took a stab at industrial development here by building a bulk flour unloading facility which resulted in large quantities of semolina wheat products moving through the yard daily. Also located here was a ramp used to load and unload trailers from flatcars, the Brooklyn Eastern District Terminal was the first to enter this field before any railroad on Long Island. The road's shops were also at this location, home of both the Alco diesel fleet and before 1962, the steam locomotives. The company's marine equipment also tied up here at the base of North Fifth and Sixth Streets. The need for rail service by the customers deteriorated from daily in the early seventies to three days a week as the eighties dawned and when no increase of business could be seen in the future, a decision had to be made. This resulted in the shut down of the entire facility on August 17, 1983.

On May 3, 1936 the Brooklyn Eastern District Terminal ("BEDT") contracted with the City of New York to provide rail service to the Wallabout Market which was adjacent to the Wallabout Basin. This was an interesting accomplishment as no less than five trunk line railroads had terminals in the Wallabout Basin area. The BEDT joined several major trunk line railroads in the Wallabout Basin area that had pier head stations; only the Lackawanna and the BEDT had trackage in Wallabout. The new City owned trackage to the Wallabout Market remained in service for only a few years when the entire area was annexed to the Brooklyn Naval Yard in December 1941. At about the same time the Brooklyn Eastern District Terminal took over all carfloat deliveries to the Navy Yard.

BEDT number 7 switching a Pennsylvania Railroad hopper car within the Kent Avenue complex in January 1940.

The conversion of the Brooklyn Navy Yard from a defense facility to a civilian industrial estate after 1960 gave the Brooklyn Eastern District an additional port of call. The small amount of trackage here, for which the Navy had utilized its own equipment, was operated on an 'as needed' basis. Service has continued past the life of the Brooklyn Eastern District Terminal Railway by the New York Cross Harbor lasting until circa 1985.

According to some sources the Brooklyn Eastern District Terminal had a facility at the base of Warren Street in Jersey City from 1910 to 1924. Havemeyer and Elder had a sugar refinery there which burned on November 24, 1924. The fire originated in the Battielle and Renwick Saltpeter Company and spread to the American Sugar Refining Company facility at 174 Washington Street, Jersey City. The 'Sugar House fire' is considered one of the two largest fires ever fought by the Jersey City Fire Department. Perhaps the BEDT was working more as a contract switching line than as a common carrier in the Garden State.

Another view of the number 7 negotiating the special work in the Kent Avenue complex on June 31, 1947. The track map suggests that this is the foot of North 9th Street.

THE SHORTLINE RAILROADS OF LONG ISLAND

The road's financial fortunes had long been tied to the fate of industrial northern Brooklyn and as that began to decline in the late sixties, so did the rail line. Indeed, if the interests that owned the New York Dock Company had not purchased all of the stock of the Brooklyn Eastern District Terminal in 1973, the road might have been abandoned in that year.

Another blow to the property came with the formation of Conrail on April 1, 1976. The big blue boys from Philadelphia were no longer interested in operating marine facilities in New York Harbor so the Terminal was in danger of losing all of its interchange as it did not physically connect with any other line. The Brooklyn Eastern District Terminal first began negotiations with the Long Island Rail Road on the possibility of acquiring the Long Island City float docks which were due to be shut down with the onslaught of Conrail. The plucky little road approached Conrail about taking over a portion of the former Pennsylvania Railroad Greenville facility in New Jersey. The deal that was inked was with Conrail and the Brooklyn Eastern District Terminal through an operating lease became a two state shortline. Besides being a two state shortline, the road also had the distinction of being an all steam locomotive property until 1962. And this was in a City that had practically banned the use of coal burning steam locomotives since 1928!

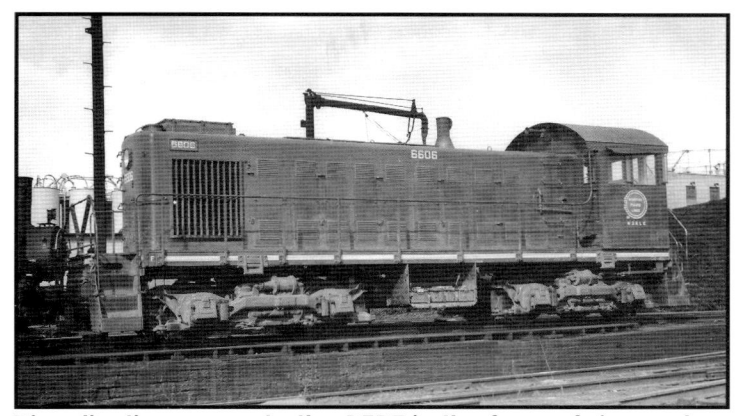

Dieselization came to the BEDT in the form of six used Alco model S-1 diesel electric locomotives. Here is the former Missouri Pacific 6606 which will become the BEDT 24 standing at the pit at North 10th Street.

By 1962 the road was operating five oil burning dual controlled steam locomotives. Then it purchased three Alco S-1 diesel locomotives from the Missouri Pacific Railroad and found that since the internal combustion locomotives lacked dual controls, firemen were needed for the diesels! A number of the people hired at this time were former Long Island Rail Road employees. The road subsequently acquired three additional diesel locomotives. A box car was acquired and painted red white and blue in 1976 to mark the celebration of the nation's two hundredth birthday. The road also put a red stripe on the already blue and white diesel 25. The lines marine equipment had usually consisted of three tug boats and several three track carfloat barges. None of the roads float dock facilities had overhead cranes for aligning the bridge until the road leased a portion of the Greenville yard in New Jersey.

We have already mentioned the shut down of the road's Williamsburg core on August 17, 1983. This marked the end of the property in the traditional sense. However, the management of the New York Dock Company which was also in the process of being shut down, purchased both it and the Brooklyn Eastern District Terminal reorganizing the enterprise as the New York Cross Harbor Railroad. There would be no rebirth of Pigeon Street or Williamsburg by the new owners, there was simply no economic reason, but the Navy Yard and the locomotive roster were to prove of some value to the new company. Indeed, the Brooklyn Navy Yard became a very hot rail property when New York Rail Car located there and became a major rail passenger car rebuilding shop for a while. Two of the diesel locomotives and parts of two others would serve the new masters. While the body of the Brooklyn Eastern District Terminal has passed away, its spirit still resides with us.

This section on the Brooklyn Eastern District Terminal began with an image of steam in the Pigeon Street terminal in Long Island City so it seems only fitting to include an internal combustion locomotive photograph in the same area. The BEDT 21 was captured by Jeff Erlitz on June 15, 1973.

'Coming around the bend' along the shore of the East River is the 22. Across the river in the background lies Manhattan which overshadows much of the Brooklyn – Queens industrial waterfront. Towering over Manhattan in this view above the locomotive is the World Trade Center, doomed to be destroyed on September 11, 2001. This image was taken on June 4, 1976 by Jeff Erlitz.

- * * * -

BROOKLYN EASTERN DISTRICT TERMINAL

Note that all equipment on hand between 1875 and 1906 was the property of the East River Terminal Company which had previously been known as the Palmer's Dock Company.

CLASS	NUMBER	BUILDER	SERIAL	DATE
	None	Baldwin Locomotive Works	3801	12/1875

This is a 0-4-0T steam 'dummy' locomotive with 17x24 cylinders and 45 inch diameter drivers named "*Frederick Havemeyer*", scrapped between 1927 and 1933.

	2	Baldwin Locomotive Works	7596	5/1885
	3	Baldwin Locomotive Works	8746	8/1887
	4	Baldwin Locomotive Works	11439	12/1890
	5	Baldwin Locomotive Works	11982	6/1891

These were four 0-4-0T steam dummy type of locomotives with 17x24 cylinders and 46 inch diameter drivers, named "*Florence*", "*Grace*", "*Lily*", and "*Arthur*"; all were scrapped between 1927 and 1933.

| | 6 | Baldwin Locomotive Works | 14743 | 3/1896 |

This is a 0-4-0T steam dummy type of locomotive with 17x24 cylinders and 46 inch diameter drivers, named "*Ethel*". This locomotive was rebuilt as a normal side tank type switch locomotive during 1918 and was scrapped by 1936.

A rear view of the number 7 sitting at the shops at North 10th Street taken on December 13, 1946.

| | 7 | Baldwin Locomotive Works | 18145 | 9/1900 |

This is a 0-6-0T tank locomotive named "*Chester*" with 17x24 cylinders and 46 inch diameter drivers. This locomotive was rebuilt as a normal side tank type switch locomotive on an unknown date and was scrapped after January 1947.

| | 9 | Baldwin Locomotive Works | 29543 | 11/1906 |

This is a 0-6-0T tank locomotive with 19x24 cylinders and 46 inch diameter drivers, retired between 1934 and 1936.

| | 10 | Baldwin Locomotive Works | 39696 | 4/1913 |

This is a 0-6-0T tank locomotive with 19x24 cylinders and 46 inch diameter drivers, cut up at the Shops in April 1963.

BROOKLYN EASTERN DISTRICT TERMINAL (continued)

The number 10 on May 31, 1937 with the BEDT logo that many railfans have used as a basis to speculate that the BEDT was founded by the Erie Railway. There is no known financial connection between the BEDT and the Erie.

The number 11 appears in this May 31, 1937 image from Harold Fagerberg. Unfortunately the location of this image has not been recorded.

| 11 | Baldwin Locomotive Works | 55276 | 1/1922 |

This is a 0-6-0T tank locomotive with 19x24 cylinders and 46 inch diameter drivers, cut up at the Shops in July 1962.

| 12 | H.K. Porter Co | 6368 | 4/1919 |

This is a 0-6-0T tank locomotive with 18x24 cylinders and 46 inch diameter drivers that was built as U.S. Navy Fleet Supply Base – South Brooklyn 3, sold to Brooklyn Eastern District Terminal during 1922 becoming 12, sold to Ron Ziel[1] in July 1963, resold March 1971 to an individual in Florida who moved it around quite a bit, donated to the Florida Gulf Coast Railroad Museum in Tampa, Florida during 1982.

The number 12 at an unknown location on May 31, 1937.

The number 13 at Pigeon Street in Long Island City on May 22, 1946.

| 13 | H.K. Porter Co | 6369 | 4/1919 |

This is a 0-6-0T tank locomotive with 18x24 cylinders and 46 inch diameter drivers that was built as U.S. Navy Fleet Supply Base – South Brooklyn 4, sold to Brooklyn Eastern District Terminal during 1922 becoming 13, sold to George Hart July 1963 for his Rail Tours Incorporated, relocated to Strasburg, Pennsylvania and acquired by the Commonwealth of Pennsylvania in January 1977 for preservation. The former 13 was subsequently resold during January 2011 to a private owner in Ohio for potential restoration.

---

[1] The immediate post BEDT ownership of the 12 and the 15 are shown as per the records of Harold Fagerberg, there has been some discussion that the ownership was actually the reverse of that shown.

THE SHORTLINE RAILROADS OF LONG ISLAND

BROOKLYN EASTERN DISTRICT TERMINAL (continued)

CLASS	NUMBER	BUILDER	SERIAL	DATE
	14	H.K. Porter Co	6260	8/1920

This is a 0-6-0T tank locomotive with 18x24 cylinders and 46 inch diameter drivers built as Mesta Machine Works 5 in West Homestead, Pennsylvania; sold to the Birmingham Rail and Locomotive Company in January 1932 and to the Brooklyn Eastern District Terminal as their 14 in February 1935, sold to George Hart in July 1963 for his Rail Tours Incorporated. This locomotive was leased to the Black River and Western Railroad but not used; sold to the Delaware and Ulster Railroad in the late 1980's and is the subject of a cosmetic restoration project.

This image of the 14 is listed as being taken in the Wallabout Market area during the 1920's. Since this facility did not open until May 3, 1936 (and closed during 1941) it appears that it has been misdated.

This image of the 15 is listed as being at the Pigeon Street terminal in Long Island City and was taken on May 11, 1950. The building visible over the pilot suggests the Kent Avenue complex however.

| | 15 | H.K. Porter Co | 5966 | 3/1917 |

This is a 0-6-0T tank locomotive with 18x24 cylinders and 46 inch diameter drivers built as Mesta Machine Works number unknown in West Homestead, Pennsylvania; sold to Brooklyn Eastern District Terminal on an unknown date becoming 15, sold to Ed Bernard[2] in July 1963 and then to the Southern Appalachia Railway in Burnsville, North Carolina in May 1965, resold to the Toledo, Lake Erie and Western Railroad in April 1975 as their 15; stored in Grand Rapids, Ohio on an unknown date. Sold during 1998 to the Strasburg Railroad who rebuilt the locomotive to resemble "Thomas the Tank Locomotive" by April 29, 1999.

Number 15 in a Gene Collora image from May 13, 1959 at Pigeon Street, Long Island City.

The number 16 standing on a float bridge apron in an undated image.

---

[2] Ibid.

BROOKLYN EASTERN DISTRICT TERMINAL (continued)

CLASS	NUMBER	BUILDER	SERIAL	DATE
	16	H.K. Porter Co	6780	1/1923

This is a 0-6-0T tank locomotive with 18x24 cylinders and 46 inch diameter drivers built as Astoria Power and Light 5, sold on an unknown date to the Fleischman Yeast Company in Peekskill, New York, number unknown. This locomotive was resold to the Brooklyn Eastern District Terminal in January 1939 via the Birmingham Rail and Locomotive Company. Sold July 1963 to George Foster, subsequently to the real estate company who had purchased the shop area of the Brooklyn Eastern District Terminal Railway property until 1988 when it was threatened with scrapping as the owner failed to remove it from the property. This locomotive was acquired by the Railroad Museum of Long Island in Riverhead, New York.

	21	Alco-GE	74351	8/1947

This was a model S1 (E1530) diesel switcher built by the American Locomotive Company ("Alco") with General Electric Company ("GE") components built as Union Railway 453, sold during 1962 to Duffy (a dealer), resold to Silicott (a dealer) who resold the unit to the Brooklyn Eastern District Terminal in 1962. Retired August 17, 1983 but acquired by the New York Cross Harbor in March 1985 as their 21. This locomotive was taken out of service during 1991 and was considered for conversion to a slug unit but was scrapped in July 2006.

The brand new (to the BEDT!) number 21 at North 10th Street; one of the steam locomotives it replaced is to its' rear.

The former Missouri Pacific 6604 still carrying those number boards; it will soon become the BEDT's number 22.

	22	Alco-GE	75525	10/1947
	23	Alco-GE	75526	10/1947
	24	Alco-GE	75527	10/1947

These were model S1 (E1530) diesel switchers built by the American Locomotive Company ("Alco") with General Electric Company ("GE") components built as New Orleans and Lower Coast 9013 to 9015, becoming Missouri Pacific 6604 to 6606 during 1961. Sold during 1962 to Duffy (a dealer), resold to Silicott (a dealer); who resold the units to the Brooklyn Eastern District Terminal in November 1962. All three locomotives were retired as of August 17, 1983 but the 22 was acquired by the New York Cross Harbor after August 17, 1983 as their 22; removed from service during 1993 and scrapped in July 2006. The 23 is believed to have been scrapped in January 1986 after being stripped for parts. The 24 was subsequently acquired by the New York Cross Harbor circa 1985 for parts and was scrapped in January 1986.

BROOKLYN EASTERN DISTRICT TERMINAL (continued)

CLASS	NUMBER	BUILDER	SERIAL	DATE

The 23 standing by the enginehouse in an undated image.

The 24 moving through the Kent Avenue yard complex. The four circular towers in the background are the BEDT's flour terminal.

      25   Alco-GE   74962   10/1946

This was a model S1 (E1530) diesel switcher built by the American Locomotive Company ("Alco") with General Electric Company ("GE") components built as Erie Railroad 307, to Erie Lackawanna Railroad 307 through a merger on October 17, 1960. This locomotive was sold to the Brooklyn Eastern District Terminal during 1968 becoming their 25. This locomotive was repainted red, white and blue during 1976 for the Bicentennial. Retired August 17, 1983 but acquired by the New York Cross Harbor in August 1983 as their 25. The 25 has been restored cosmetically as New York Central 8625 and used as a display piece in Riverside Park, Manhattan.

      26   Alco-GE   75354   8/1947

This was a model S1 (E1530) diesel switcher built by the American Locomotive Company ("Alco") with General Electric Company ("GE") components built as Erie Railroad 313, to Erie Lackawanna Railroad 313 through merger on October 17, 1960. This locomotive was sold on an unknown date to the American Electric Power (Muskingum Electric Railway) as construction locomotive 313, it was resold during 1973 to the Brooklyn Eastern District Terminal as their 26 through Silicott (a dealer). This locomotive was retired August 17, 1983 but was subsequently acquired by the New York Cross Harbor circa 1985 as a parts source; it was scrapped in January 1986.

Painted in a red, white, and blue scheme for the nation's Bicentennial, the 25 poses in front of 151 Kent Avenue in this Jeff Erlitz image taken on June 2, 1976.

The highest number on the BEDT roster was the number 26 which was caught in the Kent Avenue yard by the late Henry Maywald on January 28, 1976. Collection of John Scala.

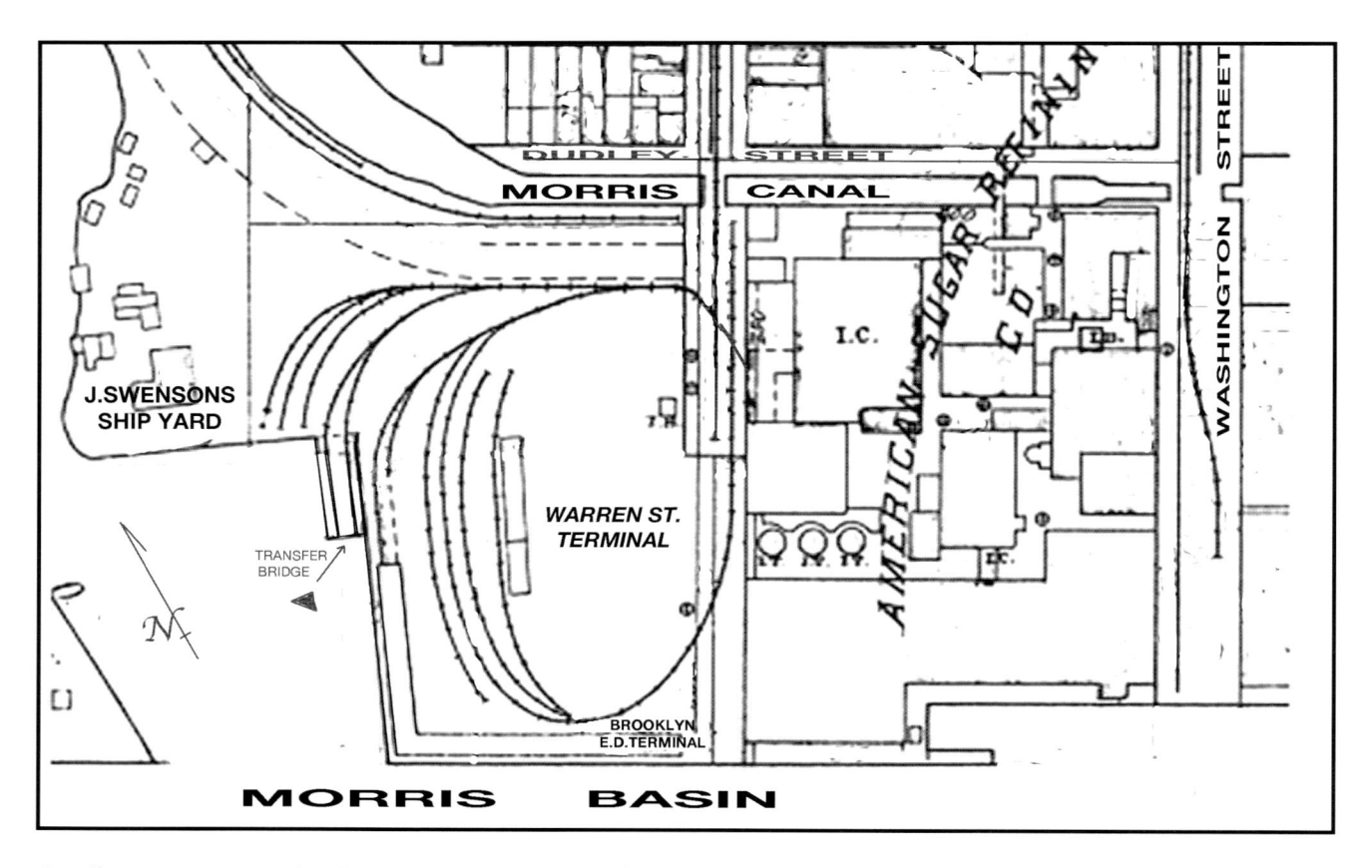

Another map re-worked by George Wybenga shows the shortlived Warren Street terminal of the Brooklyn Eastern District Terminal in Jersey City. To the right of the trackage is a rather large facility owned by the American Sugar Refining Company, a very definite clue as to why the BEDT had a facility on this side of New York harbor. Do note the lack of connections with both the Lehigh Valley Railroad in Warren Street (unmarked for clarity in the center of the diagram and the Pennsylvania Railroad in Washington Street (on the right of the map).

- * * * -

THE IMMORTAL SHORTLINE OF DIESELDOM
JAY STREET CONNECTING RAILROAD

- * * -

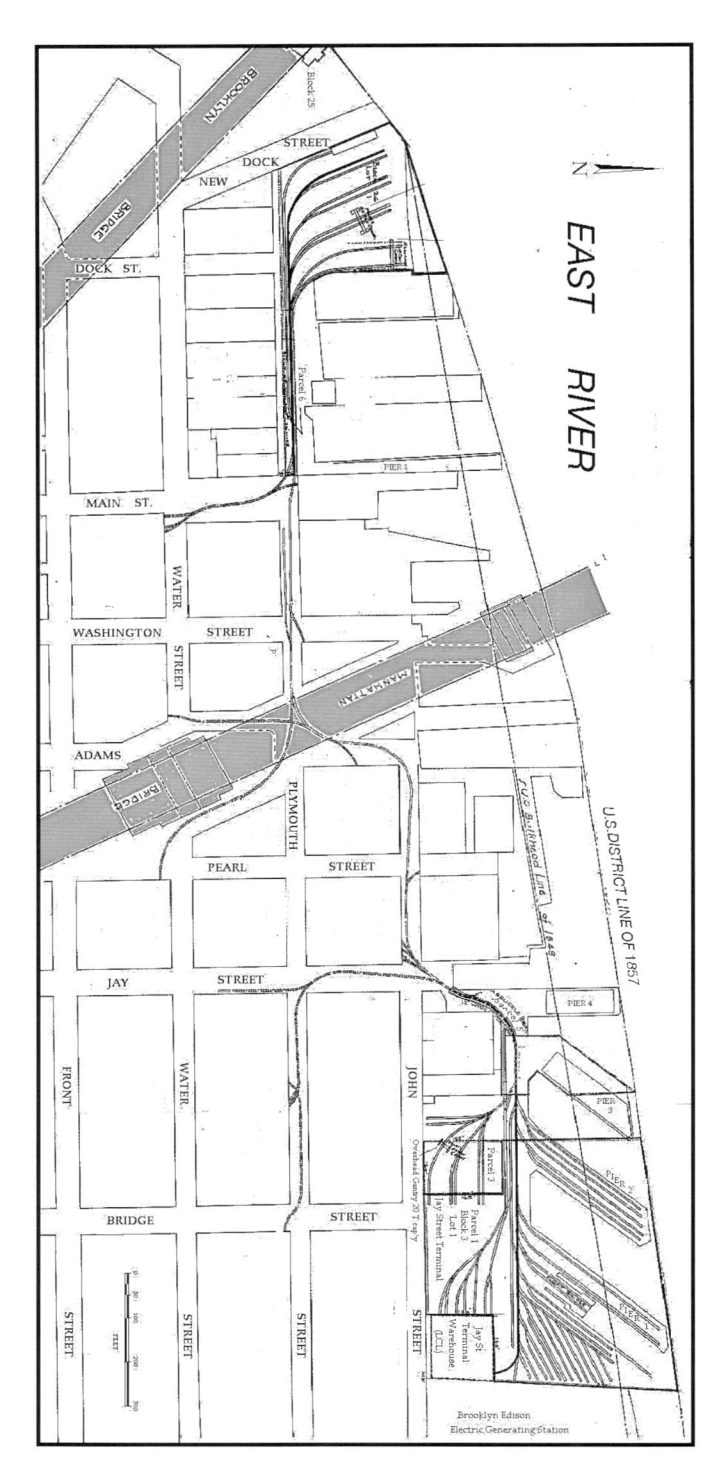

A 1944 vintage map of the area served by the Jay Street Connecting Railroad reworked by George Wybenga.

THE IMMORTAL SHORTLINE OF DIESELDOM
Jay Street Connecting Railroad

Located near a pier of the Manhattan Bridge is a patch of green grass, incongruous in its once industrial setting. This greensward and a line of derelict rails in a Brooklyn street constitute the tangible remains of the Jay Street Connecting Railroad.

The Jay Street Connecting Railroad's steamer number 1. The focus in this image is not absolutely crisp but it is a nice representation of the steam era on this railway.

The area of Brooklyn located just northwest of downtown was once known as the Arbuckle district after the Arbuckle Brothers[1], sugar and coffee merchants[2] who were once located there. Spreading along Jay Street were warehouses, a sugar refinery, a coffee roasting plant, and the necessary support facilities. At the turn of the Twentieth Century the need to link all of these operations resulted in the establishment of the Jay Street Terminal Railroad, a non common carrier who switched the Arbuckle firm's facilities. A shop, yards, and a float bridge for the interchange of cars were established down on the shore of the East River, the operating roster consisted of a tugboat, a carfloat, and a brand new (1906) Baldwin 0-6-0 side tank steam locomotive. Business was so good that an identical engine was purchased by the company during 1907.

The existence of a non common carrier is at the behest of the connecting roads and it was undoubtedly a desire to control a little more of their destiny, and a larger piece of the revenue[3]. The Arbuckle interests re-incorporated the property as the Jay Street Connecting Railroad on October 9, 1909. It was a name that would grace waybills for almost fifty years until the road was abandoned on June 27, 1959. The new entity, the Jay Street Connecting Railroad was recognized by the Interstate Commerce Committee as a common carrier after its formation.

Nine years later the road forsook steam power for new purchases when a used gas electric locomotive was purchased from the East Erie Commercial Railroad (owned by the General Electric Company) in September 1916. It would undoubtedly be interesting to examine all the factors concerning the selection of this piece of motive power, but like the locomotives building date, they have been lost to history. A search through the records of the Fire Department, City of New York does reveal that a five alarm fire was fought after an

The General Electric Company's builders photograph of the gas-electric number 3 circa 1916.

---

[1] A maternal uncle of the present author's wife (for whom she was named) was employed by the Arbuckle Brothers as a coffee taster.

[2] The Arbuckle Brothers premium brand of coffee was sold under the label 'Martinson', a brand still available today (2012).

[3] Common carrier terminal railroads in the New York Harbor zone were entitled to a minimum payment equivalent to the charge for a 75 mile line haul of a freight car.

explosion had occurred in the Arbuckle Brothers sugar refinery on April 28, 1911. Undoubtedly the fear of sparks was in the minds of the Arbuckle management.

The global strides made by internal combustion power during the First World War is only of passing interest here, but perhaps it convinced the Arbuckles to stay with the new type of railway motive power when the number 3 proved somewhat less than perfect. It was resold to General Electric as a part of a transaction that brought the Jay Street its historic immortality.

On March 17, 1917 the Jay Street Connecting Railroad became the first common carrier to order a diesel electric railroad switch engine. Delivered in October 1918 it resembled a contemporary electric steeple cab locomotive. The new number 4 suffered from prime mover problems and was returned to the manufacturer within six months. A replacement locomotive was supplied by General Electric in the form of the old Jay Street Connecting number 3, now rebuilt, in April 1919.

The 1, 2, and 3 continued to serve as a team until May 1931 when an Alco-GE-IR boxcab diesel electric locomotive that had served as a builder's demonstrator unit was received. This year old locomotive put the two steam locomotives into storage and inaugurated a new Jay Street Connecting numbering scheme; - what ever was on the unit when it arrived, it kept! Part of the land that the Jay Street Connecting Railroad operated on was sold to a real estate firm around 1941; these same interests acquired stock ownership of the line during 1945.

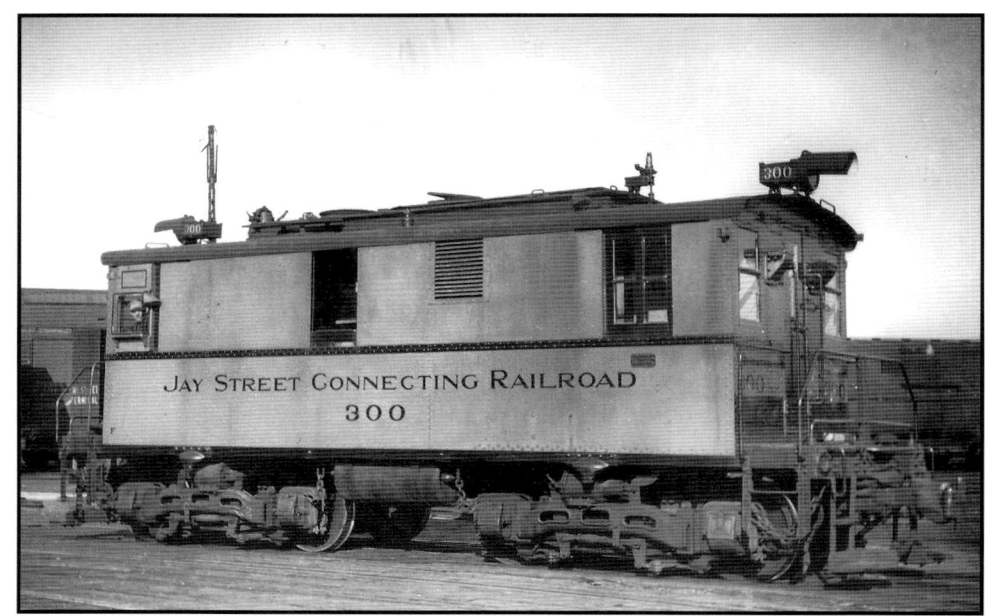

This American Locomotive Company ("Alco") boxcab was built with electrical gear by the General Electric ("GE") Company and originally served as a demonstrator numbered 300. After fifteen months in its original role it was sold to the Jay Street Connecting Railway in May 1931 retaining the number 300. This image dates from November 14, 1949. It served in Brooklyn until the road shut down.

No further changes to the roster occurred until after World War II when a one of a kind Vulcan diesel locomotive was acquired from the War Assets Administration during 1947. The former U.S. Army Transportation Corps 7511 retired the venerable number 3 which was cut down to the frame to serve as a float reacher car.

The former U.S. Army Transportation Corps 7511 after its 1947 acquisition by the Jay Street Connecting Railroad. This image dates from September 9, 1949.

The nearest the Jay Street ever got to a production diesel model came in December 1955 when an Alco C0-HH three hundred horsepower end cab switcher was acquired from the U.S. Navy who had used it at their Mare Island Shipyard in California. It received the Jay Street's orange paint with black lettering and retained its number 5. This engine only lasted in service down the middle of Adam, John, Plymouth and Jay Streets for six months. Changing traffic patterns saw loads being transferred from boxcars into trucks right at the river front float bridge after June 1956.

The remaining roster, engines 5, 300, and 7511 with the float reacher car made from the old number 3 were all put into storage until the road was abandoned on June 27, 1959. The abandonment was opposed by the remaining consignees along the line, but the Jay Street Connecting Railroad was history. Within a month all but the 7511 were sold to a Baltimore scrap dealer, where two of the engines would serve as yard switchers for five more years. The 7511 went to a gravel pit in Bound Brook, New Jersey where it lasted until 1966.

In an undated photograph the former Mare Island Navy Yard Freight Number 5 moving a Northern Pacific boxcar down Plymouth Street.

Most of the track in the cobblestone streets would last longer in abandonment than it had in revenue service.

- * * * -

JAY STREET CONNECTING RAILROAD

CLASS	NUMBER	BUILDER	SERIAL	DATE
	1	**Baldwin Locomotive Works**	27255	1/1906

This is a 0-6-0ST side tank steam locomotive with 19x24 cylinders and 46 inch diameter drivers delivered new as Jay Street Terminal Railroad 1, to Jay Street Connecting Railroad 1 through a re-incorporation of the property on October 9, 1909. The 1 was stored during 1930; it was sold during 1931 to the New York Dock Company as their 41, which was scrapped during 1951.

| | 2 | **Baldwin Locomotive Works** | 30480 | 3/1907 |

This is a 0-6-0ST side tank steam locomotive with 19x24 cylinders and 46 inch diameter drivers delivered new as Jay Street Terminal Railroad 2, to Jay Street Connecting Railroad 2 through a re-incorporation of the property on October 9, 1909. The 2 was stored during 1930, it was scrapped during 1939.

| | 3 | **General Electric** | 3765 | circa 8/1913 |

This was the second gasoline electric locomotive built by the General Electric Company. It was built as East Erie Commercial Railroad[4] 1006 and was intended to serve as a demonstrator unit. The locomotive consisted of a Union Iron Works carbody sheltering a GM-16C6 prime mover on an Erie Steel Construction Company frame with four General Electric model 205D traction motors in Wason trucks. This locomotive was acquired by the Jay Street Connecting Railroad in September 1916 but was resold to the General Electric Company due to mechanical issues in August 1918. This locomotive became East Erie Commercial Railroad first number 2 and was rebuilt with model HM-820A traction motors. This locomotive was leased to the U.S. Army for use at the Aberdeen Proving Grounds in Maryland as their E-1 from October 1918 until January 1919. The locomotive was again sold to the Jay Street Connecting Railroad in April 1919 resuming the number 3 on the roster. Retired during 1948, this locomotive was cut down to the frame and trucks for use as a float reacher car. Stored in June 1956 and cut up for scrap by the Patapsco Scrap Company in Brooklyn during May 1959.

| | 4 | **General Electric** | 6206 | 9/1918 |

This was the first diesel electric locomotive switch engine on a common carrier railroad in the United States. The Union Iron Works carbody sheltered a GM-50 prime mover on an Erie Steel Construction Company frame with Wason trucks. This pioneering locomotive was returned to General Electric with prime mover problems in April 1919. Rebuilt during 1922 with a Sterling Dolphin prime mover, it became East Erie Commercial Railroad second 2. This locomotive was dismantled for parts in August 1934. The frame, trucks, and cab were used to construct East Erie Commercial Railroad 11 in March 1936; this locomotive was wrecked in August 1940 and retired.

| | 5 | **Alco – GE** | 68690 | 6/1935 |

This was a B-B trucked model Co-HH end cab diesel switcher with a Mac Intosh and Seymour prime mover. It was built by the American Locomotive Company ("Alco") with electrical gear by the General Electric ("GE") Company. It was built as Navy Yard Freight 5, a military switching line serving the U.S. Navy's Mare Island Shipyard in California. This locomotive was also assigned 65-00451 in the U.S. Navy's service wide locomotive roster but this number may not have been carried by the locomotive. The Jay Street Connecting Railroad acquired this locomotive in December 1955 from the Naval Ammunition Depot in Hingham, Massachusetts; it retained the number 5 on the Jay Street Connecting. This locomotive was stored serviceable in June 1956 and sold to the Patapsco Scrap Company in May 1959 who moved the unit to Baltimore and utilized it as a yard switcher until July 1964 when it was cut up for scrap.

---

[4] The East Erie Commercial Railroad is a common carrier that is also the 'in-house' terminal railway line serving the General Electric plant in East Erie, Pennsylvania.

THE SHORTLINE RAILROADS OF LONG ISLAND

JAY STREET CONNECTING RAILROAD (connecting)

CLASS	NUMBER	BUILDER	SERIAL	DATE
	300	Alco – GE	68488	8/1930

This was a B-B trucked 300 horsepower boxcab locomotive that was mechanically similar to the 5. This locomotive was built by the <u>A</u>merican <u>L</u>ocomotive <u>Co</u>mpany ("Alco") with electrical gear by the <u>G</u>eneral <u>E</u>lectric ("GE") Company for service as a demonstrator numbered 300. After fifteen months in its original role it was sold to the Jay Street Connecting Railroad in May 1931. This locomotive was stored serviceable in June 1956 and sold to the Patapsco Scrap Company in May 1959 who moved the unit to Baltimore and utilized it as a yard switcher until July 1964 when it was cut up for scrap.

| | 7511 | Vulcan Iron Works | 4394 | 2/1944 |

This was a B-B trucked sixty ton center cab switch locomotive with a Buda 6DH-1897 prime mover built as United States Army Transportation Corps 7511 and used at Fort Hancock, Maryland. This locomotive was acquired by the Jay Street Connecting Railroad during 1947 from the War Assets Administration. This locomotive was stored serviceable in June 1956 and it was sold to the Houdaille Construction Company in Bound Brook, New Jersey where it worked as the 7511 in a gravel pit until it was scrapped in March 1966.

The old Jay Street Connecting Railroad number 3 apparently while being converted to a float reach car on October 19, 1949.

- * * * -

HOOD UNITS, BOXCARS AND BUILDINGS

BUSH TERMINAL RAILROAD

- * * -

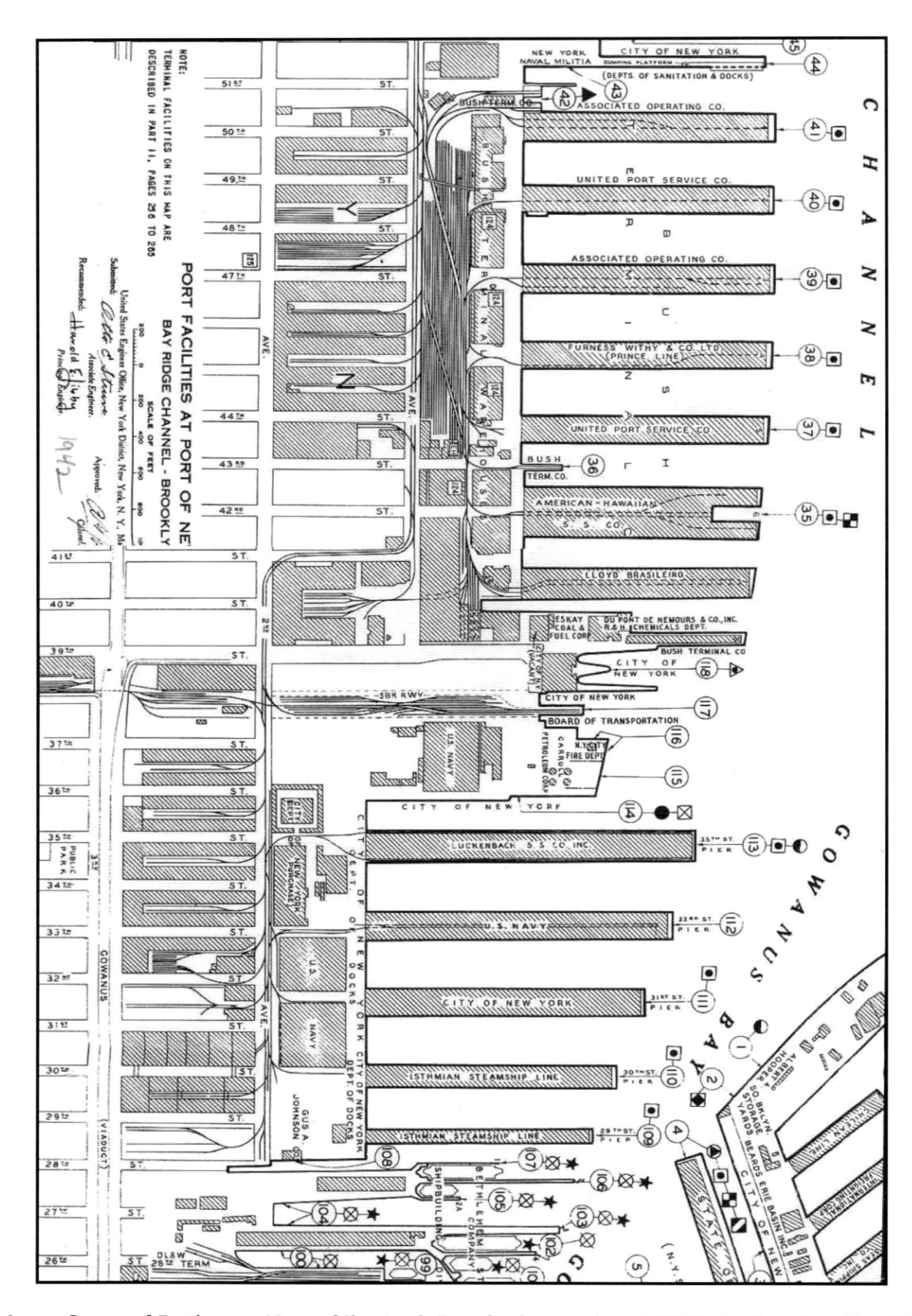

A U.S. Army Corps of Engineers Map of the Bush Terminal area dated 1942. Notice that Pier 117 is labeled City of New York, Board of Transportation. This was the pier used to land the R1 through R9 cars of the Independent Subway Line; the railway running to the east (left in the map) is the South Brooklyn Railway which connected at this point. Also on the bottom edge of the map is the Lackawanna's 25th Street Terminal.

HOOD UNITS, BOXCARS AND BUILDINGS
BUSH TERMINAL RAILROAD

Irving T. Bush had a dream of an industrial utopia located in South Brooklyn. The fruition of these ideas changed the landscape of a good part of the New York Harbor waterfront. This area saw some very early diesel railway locomotives go into common carrier service, a trolley passenger line; and this was just in the first thirty years of the company's existence!

Some of the negatives in the Fagerberg collection have not fared well through the years such as this image of the Bush Terminal enginehouse in the days of steam locomotives. From left to right appear the 6, 4, 2, 5, and 3; all are Baldwin built 0-4-0T's and were the first to carry these numbers on the road. Note the lettering 'Bush Docks' on the side tanks of the 5 and the 3.

The Bush Terminal Company was incorporated in the state of New York on February 10, 1902 to acquire two hundred acres of land on the Brooklyn waterfront with the intention of constructing a railway terminal and warehouse properties on it. In December 1904 the corporation transferred the real property of the enterprise to a subsidiary, the Bush Terminal Company, Limited[1]. In January 1905 all of the stock of the subsidiary Bush Terminal Railroad and the subsidiary Bush Land Company not then in the hands of the Bush Terminal Company was acquired.

Erected on the two hundred acre premises were fifteen reinforced concrete loft buildings that over a century later are still a distinctive architectural feature on that portion of the Brooklyn landscape. Along with these six to eight story structures there were constructed over one hundred smaller individual warehouse units and eight piers jutting out into New York harbor. Between all of the buildings there were more than thirty million cubic feet of industrial area. In addition to this industrial complex an office building on the south side at 130 to 132 West 42nd Street between Sixth and Seventh Avenues in Manhattan was constructed during 1916[2]. The Bush idea behind the office building was to have available to its Brooklyn industrial occupants an office and showroom space in New York City. To move raw materials and products into and around these facilities the Bush Terminal Company built a switching railroad to serve the property. A large portion of the eighteen miles of track was installed in First Avenue, Second Avenue and Forty-First Street. Even a 'tunnel' of sorts graced this rail operation; a railway curve was built through the corner frontage of a structure located at Second Avenue and Forty-First Street. The original operation was with small 0-4-0 steam tank locomotives, one built in each year from 1901 to 1903 with the final two coming in 1904. The locomotives moved cars from both the float bridge on the harbor and from an interchange with the Long Island Rail Road's Bay Ridge Branch to the numerous delivery points throughout Bush Terminal. There was also an interchange with the South Brooklyn Railroad on the north side of the property.

---

[1] The use of the term 'Limited' in this firm is deliberate; the Bush Terminal Company was attempting to develop an office building in London, England at the time.
[2] This building was lost to the Bush Terminal Company through foreclosure during 1938.

The street trackage and a portion of the yard trackage was electrified with a 600 volt direct current overhead trolley wire starting in 1905. This was used by a second hand steeplecab locomotive that was delivered to the property at about this time. Part of the line on Second Avenue was utilized by the Brooklyn Rapid Transit for their trolley car operations. The Bush Terminal also got into the passenger business, rather unusual for a terminal switching line. Taking advantage of the trolley wire, a ten window semi-convertible car was ordered from the J.G. Brill Company and numbered 1. The route of the trolley car appears to have been from the Thirty-Ninth Street ferry terminal at the water's edge, turning south into First Avenue which was followed to Fifty-First Street. This line would have acted as a commuter line for workers in the Bush Terminal loft buildings coming from Manhattan and for those who had taken a trolley from elsewhere in Brooklyn down to the ferry terminal.

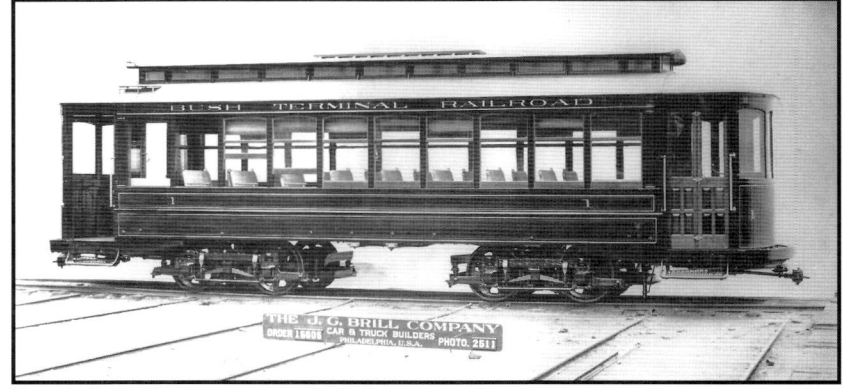

The J.G. Brill Company builder's photograph of trolley car first 1 taken as it was leaving the builder in 1906.

This limited electric operation appears to have been done basically for smoke abatement purposes, but it was successful enough that the Bush Terminal Railroad added an additional electric locomotive in 1907; and two additional steeplecab electrics in 1911 and 1916. The steam locomotive roster was also added to in the interim with three more locomotives, two 0-4-0T's from Baldwin in 1910 and 1916; with one from Alco-Cooke in 1915.

While we are looking at the motive power acquisitions, there is a transaction that very little is known about. On March 16, 1903 the Bush Terminal Railroad is recorded as purchasing two former Manhattan Elevated 'Forney' type steam locomotives, the former Elevated 88 was supposedly for the Brooklyn operation, but there is no further record of it. The second little 0-4-4-T, the former 77 was earmarked for the 'Bush Terminal, Jersey City' but there are no further records of the locomotive or any further enterprise in Jersey City. Perhaps the 88 was used to construct the property in Brooklyn and then disposed of, not an unknown use for an old Manhattan Elevated steam locomotive.

Electric locomotive number 22 had been built as the number 10 and went on to a second career in Canada as the number 91 of the Hudson Bay Mining Company. This image was taken November 1, 1931.

The locomotive roster of the Bush Terminal Railroad is very stable from 1911 until after the start of the Great Depression. Basically Bush Terminal delivered a car to their consignees. When it was reloaded or empty, the car went back to the float bridge or to the Long Island Rail Road. For variety there was an occasional interchange load for the South Brooklyn Railway at Thirty-Ninth Street. The operation would remain the same after September 1931 but the motive power would not.

The City of New York had legislated coal burning locomotives out of the City and the eight four wheeled tank locomotives on the Bush Terminal Railroad were ready targets. The extension of the already in place electrification did not appear to be an available solution but the 'new fangled' motive power being used at 25th Street, Brooklyn by the Delaware, Lackawanna and Western Railroad was. The Bush Terminal sat down with the American Locomotive Company – General Electric – Ingersoll Rand consortium and liked what it saw mechanically but realized that a boxcab was a terrible design to be used in switching service. The result of the engineering work was a landmark design, the first 'hood' style diesel electric locomotive, as well as the first multiple order for 'oil-electrics' to date. These seven new locomotives served masterfully, replacing the eight steam locomotives immediately and the trolley wire came down circa 1939[3]. The seven diesel locomotives took over these additional duties without the need for any additional extra motive power during the very busy days of World War II. The eventual fate of the steam locomotives is not known, but the subsequent histories of the steeplecabs; to the extent that it is known, is presented in the accompanying roster.

We should pause now and look back at the passenger service. During the World War I period the Bush Terminal's trolley car was also allowed to operate down the Brooklyn Rapid Transit's track in Second Avenue as far south as Sixty-Third Street but this appears to have been only a temporary wartime operation. The line reverted to service only on First Avenue after September 26, 1919. The original car 1 was reportedly no longer fit for service after 1923 so the Bush Terminal Railroad reportedly began to lease cars from the Brooklyn Rapid Transit system[4]. After a four year period of dealing with rented cars, the Bush Terminal purchased a single 'Birney' type car that had been built as a demonstrator from a line in Connecticut. This car had a short six year life among the warehouses and it was retired in September 1933. After a two month hiatus a 'Birney' car was purchased from the South Brooklyn Railway and it served as the third number 1 until passenger service was discontinued in July 1934.

The pioneering hood units continued in service day in and day out for over thirty years unassisted. The same could not be said for their corporate parent. The Bush Terminal Company[5] sold off the majority of it's buildings to the City of New York on June 10, 1963 with the property becoming known as Industry City. The Bush Terminal Railroad continued to serve the premises, but the locomotives were getting old and tired. The line picked up two former military locomotives in 1956 and 1962 respectively, and began to remove the oil-electrics from service during 1964.

The diesel numbered second number 5 still sporting its' original paint scheme moves from the yard out into the street in this undated photograph. The motor vehicles in the view suggest it was taken in the late 1940's.

---

[3] During the delivery of the City of New York's Independent Subway line R-1 cars in 1932 these cars were unloaded at a float bridge using a Plymouth diesel mechanical locomotive numbered 10. This locomotive was a demonstrator owned by the Fate-Roote-Heath (Plymouth) firm and apparently was leased by the City of New York for this endeavor.

[4] See Appendix I for a list of the known leased cars.

[5] The Bush Terminal Company corporate charter was eventually acquired by the Hamilton Watch Company.

When both the railroad and the buildings had been in the same hands the business on the rail line had been good, but the city with its' adjacent Brooklyn-Queens Expressway began to emphasize delivery by truck and the railcar loadings began to diminish. The result was the abandonment of the Bush Terminal Railroad line on December 31, 1971, with the last foreign line cars being handled on January 1, 1972. However, a directed service order was issued by the Interstate Commerce Commission in April 1972 and the line was operated by the New York Dock Railway primarily using the Bush Terminal Company's 88 and 89 until the remains of the Bush Terminal Railway were merged into the New York Dock Company in January 1975.

One of the more interesting attributes of the Bush Terminal Railway was the double track 'tunnel' under the building on the northwest corner of Second Avenue and Forty-First Street. While the northern portion of the old Bush Terminal property has not seen rail service for many years, the 'tunnel' was still there to be photographed on April 7, 2012 by Edward M. Koehler Jr.

Trouble at the 'tunnel'! The driver of that Cadillac on the left has parked his car so it fouls the Bush Terminal trackage. Sperry railcar 402 was making its' way from the South Brooklyn Railway interchange to the Bush Terminal floats when an alert train crew halted all progress. This incident was captured by Benjamin W. Schaeffer on January 29, 1979.

- * * * -

BUSH TERMINAL RAILROAD

CLASS	NUMBER	BUILDER	SERIAL	DATE

Trolley Cars
      first 1   **J.G. Brill Co**   15605   __/1906

This was a double truck semi-convertible trolley car with an unknown seating capacity; it was off of the roster by 1923.

      second 1   **Saint Louis Car Co**   1188   __/1927

This was a single truck 'Birney' car, probably seating thirty-two, that had been a demonstrator for the Saint Louis Car Company. This car was later sold to the Danbury and Bethel Power and Transportation Company but was apparently not used or numbered on that line. This car was sold to the Bush Terminal Company as their second 1 during 1927 and is believed to have been out of service by May 1933.

The second trolley car to carry the number 1 is seen here appearing semi-derelict at the engine house. To its rear, based on its Brooklyn Rapid Transit style paint scheme is the third number 1. Further to the rear is one of the Alco – General Electric – Ingersoll Rand diesels.

      third 1   **Cincinnati**   2395   3/1919

This was a single truck 'Birney' car, probably seating thirty-two that had been built as South Brooklyn Railway (Brooklyn Rapid Transit) 7203. This car was sold to the Bush Terminal Company during 1933 and is believed to have been retired after the end of passenger service in July 1934.

Locomotives
      first 2   **Baldwin Locomotive Works**   19352   8/1901
      first 3   **Baldwin Locomotive Works**   20903   9/1902
      first 4   **Baldwin Locomotive Works**   22638   8/1903
      first 5   **Baldwin Locomotive Works**   23520   1/1904
      first 6   **Baldwin Locomotive Works**   23553   1/1904

These were five 0-4-0T steam tank locomotives with 18x24 cylinders and 44 inch diameter drivers; they were all retired during 1931, no further information.

This is a detail from the enginehouse picture shown earlier in this chapter, this is a closer view of the first 5 (left) and the first 3 (right).

BUSH TERMINAL COMPANY (continued)

<u>CLASS</u>   <u>NUMBER</u>   <u>BUILDER</u>   <u>SERIAL</u>   <u>DATE</u>

The number 1 switching cars in the main Bush Terminal yard in an undated image.

Another undated image showing the second number 2 in its' original paint scheme.

The second number 3 with the second number 6 behind; both it and the second number 4 (right) are in the second and final scheme applied to these locomotives.

The second number 4 moving through the yard on June 17, 1963 at a spritely forty-two years of age; it would remain in service seven more years.

1	Alco – GE – IR	11484	9/1931
second 2 to 6	Alco – GE – IR	11485 to 11488	9/1931
7	Alco – GE – IR	11489	9/1931

These were seven B-B trucked 600 horsepower 'oil-electric' locomotives that were built by a consortium of the <u>A</u>merican <u>L</u>ocomotive <u>Co</u>mpany ("Alco"), <u>G</u>eneral <u>E</u>lectric ("GE"), and <u>I</u>ngersoll <u>R</u>and ("IR"). They were the first 'hood' type diesel locomotives installed on a common carrier railroad in the United States. The 1 was retired in July 1964 and was scrapped in October 1966. The second 2 and the second 5 were retired in April 1975 and scrapped in September 1975. The second 3, second 6, and 7 were retired in March 1967 and scrapped in May 1967. The second 4 was retired in May 1970 and stored until it was scrapped in September 1975.

The number 7 standing outside of the enginehouse on July 25, 1938 with a maintenance of way push flat alongside of it.

THE SHORTLINE RAILROADS OF LONG ISLAND

PAGE 37

BUSH TERMINAL COMPANY (continued)

CLASS	NUMBER	BUILDER	SERIAL	DATE
	8	General Electric	1837	__/1904

This was a B-B trucked electric locomotive built as Dayton, Lebanon and Cincinnati number unknown, acquired by the Bush Terminal Company during 1905. This locomotive was retired circa 1941 and sold to the Public Service Coordinated Transport of New Jersey as their number 2 by 1944; no further information.

| | 9 | Alco – GE | 50094 | 7/1911 |

This was a B-B trucked electric locomotive, built by a consortium of the American Locomotive Company ("Alco") and General Electric ("GE"); the locomotive carrying General Electric builders number 3464 and built as Bush Terminal Railway 9. This locomotive was apparently numbered as 20 on an unknown date. This locomotive was sold to the Hudson Bay Mining Company as their 92 during 1941, no further information.

| | 10 | Alco – GE | 41642 | 5/1907 |

This was a B-B trucked electric locomotive, built by a consortium of the American Locomotive Company ("Alco") and General Electric ("GE"); the locomotive carrying General Electric builders number 2549, built as Bush Terminal Railway 10. It is believed that this locomotive was renumbered 22 on an unknown date. This locomotive was sold to the Hudson Bay Mining Company during 1941 becoming their 91; scrapped during 1956.

The only non Baldwin Locomotive Works steamer on the roster was the number 12 seen here in a faded builder's photograph.

	11	Baldwin Locomotive Works	34458	4/1910
	12	Alco – Cooke Works	55201	7/1915
	14	Baldwin Locomotive Works	44462	11/1916

These were three 0-4-0T steam tank locomotives with 18x24 cylinders and 44 inch drivers[6]; they were all retired during 1931, no further information.

| | 20 | Alco – GE | 50094 | 7/1911 |

This was a B-B trucked electric locomotive, built by a consortium of the American Locomotive Company ("Alco") and General Electric ("GE"); the locomotive carrying General Electric builders number 3464 and built as Bush Terminal Railway 9. This locomotive was apparently numbered as 20 on an unknown date. This locomotive was sold to the Hudson Bay Mining Company as their 92 during 1941, no further information.

---

[6] Dimensions for the 11 are assumed.

BUSH TERMINAL COMPANY (continued)

CLASS	NUMBER	BUILDER	SERIAL	DATE
	22	Alco – GE	41642	5/1907

This was a B-B trucked electric locomotive, built by a consortium of the American Locomotive Company ("Alco") and General Electric ("GE"); the locomotive carrying General Electric builders number 2549, built as Bush Terminal Railway 10. It is believed that this locomotive was renumbered 22 on an unknown date. This locomotive was sold to the Hudson Bay Mining Company during 1941 becoming their 91; scrapped during 1956.

	23	General Electric	4903	8/1914

This was a large steeplecab locomotive that was built and exhibited at the Panama Pacific Exhibit in San Francisco on behalf of General Electric. This locomotive was not delivered to the Bush Terminal Company until 1916. This locomotive was sold during 1939 to the Waterloo, Cedar Falls and Northern Railroad who rebuilt it and outshopped it as their 190 during 1940. This locomotive was severely damaged in a carbarn fire on October 31, 1954[7] and it was scrapped.

	88	General Electric	18014	7/1943

This was a B-B trucked center cab 400 horsepower diesel locomotive that had been built as United States Army Transportation Corps 7864. Acquired by the Bush Terminal Company during 1956; transferred to the New York Dock Railway in January 1974 and scrapped in March 1980.

The former United States Army Transportation Corps 7864 as Bush 88 showing off the striped paint scheme applied to it. This design probably didn't take all those louvers into account.

The Bush 89 in the more austere green paint scheme without stripes. It is coupled to a float reacher car that was built by modifying an ordinary gondola with crew access ladders at the four corners.

	89	General Electric	28241	9/1945

This was a B-B trucked center cab 400 horsepower diesel locomotive that had been built for the United States Marine Corps, its road number unknown. Acquired by the Bush Terminal Company during 1962; transferred to the New York Dock Railway in January 1974 and scrapped in March 1980.

	unknown	Baldwin Locomotive Works	4485	12/1878

This 0-4-4T 'Forney' style steam locomotive with 10x14 cylinders and 38 inch diameter drivers was built as Manhattan Elevated Railway 77; it was reportedly acquired by the Bush Terminal Company on March 16, 1903 for an operation in Jersey City. There is no further information about this locomotive or a Jersey City operation of the Bush Terminal Company.

---

[7] This was not the same fire that destroyed the former South Brooklyn Railway first number 7 which had occurred in 1950.

THE SHORTLINE RAILROADS OF LONG ISLAND

BUSH TERMINAL COMPANY (continued)

CLASS	NUMBER	BUILDER	SERIAL	DATE
	unknown	Rhode Island Locomotive	742	1/1879

This 0-4-4T 'Forney' style steam locomotive with 10x14 cylinders and 38 inch diameter drivers was built as Manhattan Elevated Railway class C1 number 88; it was reportedly acquired by the Bush Terminal Company on March 16, 1903 for use in Brooklyn. This locomotive was reportedly sold on July 20, 1907 to the Whitewater Lumber Company in Antaugaville, Alabama and then resold on March 23, 1910 to Solvay Process in Syracuse, New York. There is no further information about this locomotive. This locomotive may have been used on an early passenger service on the Bush Terminal Railway.

Note that gaps in the locomotive roster are the result of the Bush Terminal Company also numbering their automobiles and trucks in the same number series.

Finishing up our visit to the Bush Terminal Railway we have two undated images of their second number 6, the one on the left in the original paint scheme, the location is the main yard at Bush Terminal; the image on the right has this diesel pioneer posed in front of the enginehouse carrying its' final image.

This material has been focusing on the locomotives of the shortlines, but one can not forget the non revenue cars that also existed. We have already mentioned the Bush Terminal float reach car, numbered 101. It was placed into storage during the New York Dock era in the Bush Terminal. During this time, on July 31, 1980, Benjamin W. Schaeffer caught this image of it.

- * * * -

APPENDIX I

BROOKLYN RAPID TRANSIT TROLLEY CARS
LEASED TO THE BUSH TERMINAL COMPANY
1923 to 1927

Bernard Linder in his article on the Bush Terminal Company (see the bibliography) identified three cars that were leased to the Bush Terminal Company by the Brooklyn Rapid Transit and its successor the Brooklyn Manhattan Transit.

CLASS	NUMBER	BUILDER	SERIAL	DATE
	579	American Car Co	unknown	__/1898

This was a double truck closed car owned by the Brooklyn City Railroad; it was leased from July 1923 until June 1924 and again from January 1926 until June 1926. This group of cars (555 to 579) was scrapped between 1928 and 1933.

| | 2191 | Briggs Car Co | unknown | __/1899 |

This was a double truck closed car owned by the Nassau Electric Railroad; it was leased from June 1924 until July 1927. This group of cars (2175 to 2199[8]) was scrapped between 1925 and 1928.

| | 2759 | Laclede | unknown | __/1902 |

This was a double truck closed car owned by the Nassau Electric Railroad; it was leased during 1927 prior to the delivery of the trolley car second 1. This group of cars (2705 to 2799) was scrapped between 1930 and 1938.

Mr. Linder also lists the Saint Louis Car Company as building a car numbered 3 for the Bush Terminal but this car does not show up in the builder lists of the Saint Louis Car Company nor does this number appear to reconcile with the known roster.

- * * * -

---

[8] Several cars of this group were sold to the Third Avenue Railway who leased them to the Steinway Lines.

APPENDIX II

THE INDUSTRIAL RAILWAYS OF THE BUSH TERMINAL AREA

In addition to the Bush Terminal Railroad and the South Brooklyn Railway; there were two military facilities and one industry in the Bush Terminal area whom also operated railway equipment.

E.W. Bliss, Bush Terminal area[9]

The E.W. Bliss firm was incorporated during 1885 with their plant located at the foot of Adams Street. During 1890 the Bliss firm moved to what would become the Bush Terminal area in later years. This firm specialized in the manufacture of heavy equipment used to shape, drill and bend metal. A separate powerhouse to provide electricity for the factory was located north of 53rd Street and west of First Avenue; across from the E.W. Bliss Plant. At the rear of the powerhouse was a coal pocket which was fed by an elevated railroad that extended to a coal hoist located on the shore of the harbor. This firm utilized a rare battery powered locomotive to move coal hopper cars along their elevated railway. The E.W. Bliss firm relocated to plants in New Jersey and Ohio; laying off their last workers in Brooklyn during 1947.

CLASS	NUMBER	BUILDER	SERIAL	DATE
none		General Electric Co	8080	9/1920

This was a double truck 'gable hood' battery locomotive that was sold after 1947 to the Old Ben Coal Company in Princeton, Indiana who operated it with no road number. This locomotive was stored circa 1973 (with one wheel welded to the rail) on the property of the Graham Grain Company in Terre Haute, Indiana. This locomotive is believed to have been scrapped.

U.S. Army, Military Ocean Terminal, Bush Terminal area

With the entry of the United States into World War I it became a part of that effort to establish a military controlled port to support the American Expeditionary Force being sent to Europe. An undeveloped portion of the Bush Terminal property at its southern end was requisitioned around January 1, 1918. The complex was located at First Avenue and 58th Street in the Bay Ridge section of Brooklyn. A large warehouse and dock complex was constructed on the site. The warehouses and docks were linked to each other with bridges. To allow for the delivery of goods and troops to the facility, track connections were made with both the Long Island Rail Road Bay Ridge Branch on the bases' southern end and the Bush Terminal on the northern end. There were seventeen miles of trackage on the fifty-seven acres of land covered by the base. The facility had a number of separate railway yards with a total capacity of 799 freight cars with an additional 100 cars accommodated at the freight docks in the twin warehouse buildings.

An interior view of the Military Ocean Terminal after it was turned into a 'vertical' industrial park by the City of New York. Those railcars in the view are former Long Island Rail Road P72 bar generator cars turned into a lunchroom facility. Undated image from Robert Delmonico.

---

[9] The E.W. Bliss firm also had another Brooklyn location on the Jay Street Connecting Railroad where torpedoes were built for the United States Navy.

APPENDIX II – THE INDUSTRIAL RAILWAYS OF THE BUSH TERMINAL AREA (continued)

U.S. Army, Military Ocean Terminal, Bush Terminal area (continued)
After the First World War the base inventory was slimmed down but it remained in service as an Army facility. The premises were also used by German flag ocean liners and freighters which were denied any other anchorage in the port of New York[10] between the two world wars. During World War II the Military Ocean Terminal resumed its role as a supply base to the army forces in Europe. It appears that until the World War II era this facility was switched by the Bush Terminal Railway. During the World War II period the Military Ocean Terminal was assigned its own locomotive by the Army's Transportation Corps. The first locomotive was a forty-five ton diesel electric; it was later replaced with a heavier eighty ton unit. After the war a more somber duty, the return of the honored war dead became a part of this facility's duties. This final honoring of the war dead was the subject of an article in LIFE magazine. As military shipping moved to air and shipboard containers after the Korean Conflict the use of this facility diminished to closure; it was purchased by the City of New York in 1981.

CLASS	NUMBER	BUILDER	SERIAL	DATE
	7426	Fate – Root – Heath	4069	11/15/1940

This was a B-B trucked forty-five ton 300 horsepower diesel electric locomotive that was built for the U.S. Army as their 7426. This locomotive was transferred to Camp Claiborne. Louisiana on an unknown date; offered for sale by the War Assets Administration in February, 1946; no further information.

| | 7896 | General Electric Co | 18061 | 11/1943 |

This was a B-B trucked 80 ton center cab switching locomotive built new as U.S. Army 7896 and assigned to the Brooklyn Military Ocean Terminal. There is no disposition information for this locomotive.

Besides these two standard gauge locomotive, sources suggest three other locomotives owned by the U.S. Army as being associated with the base; the first is a thirty-six inch gauge Plymouth model HT2 of three and a half tons (builders number 3213 of May 17, 1929) that was ordered by the Raritan Arsenal in New Jersey and shipped to the Military Ocean Terminal. The other two are Plymouth builder numbers 3902 and 3903 of May 26 and May 27, 1937 which were eight ton model DLL2's and were of sixty inch gauge (as used in Russia, Spain, and Portugal); the author believes that all three of these locomotives were 'passing through' enroute to assignments in Europe prior to World War II.

United States Navy, South Brooklyn Fleet Supply Base, Bush Terminal area
During the First World War the United States Navy decided to use New York Harbor as the main supply base for the naval units supporting the American Expeditionary Force in Europe. The supply base was established at 830 Third Avenue between 29th Street and 32nd Street. This base opened on September 23, 1918 and consisted of two warehouse loft buildings, two warehouses, and a powerhouse. To enable supplies to reach the facility a rail yard was constructed and a fleet of four identical 0-6-0 steam locomotives were purchased. As a supply depot, this facility was probably mothballed during 1922 when it is documented two of the locomotives assigned here were sold; the other two were probably also disposed of at this time. During the First World War the base functioned as originally intended; during World War II this was the home of a Naval Clothing Supply

---

[10] The Long Island Rail Road would actually operate 'boat trains' from Pennsylvania Station New York to the pier area.

THE SHORTLINE RAILROADS OF LONG ISLAND

APPENDIX II – THE INDUSTRIAL RAILWAYS OF THE BUSH TERMINAL AREA (continued)

<u>United States Navy</u>, South Brooklyn Fleet Supply Base, Bush Terminal area (continued)
Depot. After the Second World War this facility was turned over to the General Services Administration for use as a Federal warehouse during 1960. One part of this group of structures is now occupied by a Federal Detention Center. The United States Navy assembled a fleet of four identical Portersteam tank locomotives to switch this storehouse facility which had an interchange with the Bush Terminal Railway.

CLASS	NUMBER	BUILDER	SERIAL	DATE
1		H.K. Porter Co	6366	3/1919
	2 to 4	H.K. Porter Co	6367 to 6369	4/1919

These were four 0-6-0T tank locomotives with 18x24 cylinders and 46 inch diameter drivers that were built as U.S. Navy Fleet Supply Base – South Brooklyn 1 to 4; it is believed that this base was mothballed circa 1922 and these locomotives were sold off at this date. There is no disposition information for the numbers 1 and 2. The number 3 was sold to Brooklyn Eastern District Terminal Railway during 1922 becoming 12, sold to Ron Ziel[11] in July 1963, resold March 1971 to an individual in Florida who moved it around quite a bit, donated to the Florida Gulf Coast Railroad Museum in Tampa, Florida during 1982. The number 4 was sold to Brooklyn Eastern District Terminal Railway during 1922 becoming 13, sold to George Hart July 1963 for his Rail Tours Incorporated, relocated to Strasburg, Pennsylvania and acquired by the Commonwealth of Pennsylvania in January 1977 for preservation. The former 13 was subsequently resold during January 2011 to a private owner in Ohio for potential restoration.

The former U.S. Navy Fleet Supply Base – South Brooklyn 3 in its better known civilian guise as Brooklyn Eastern District Terminal number 12. While we don't know the date of this image the locomotive is standing at the pit at the North 10th Street Shops. This locomotive now enjoys retirement in Florida.

- * * * -

---

[11] There is some dispute over the initial post Brooklyn Eastern District Terminal ownership of this locomotive, it may have been owned by Ed Bernard instead of Ron Ziel. See the Brooklyn Eastern District Terminal roster for more information.

DOWN ON THE BROOKLYN DOCKS
NEW YORK DOCK RAILWAY

- * * -

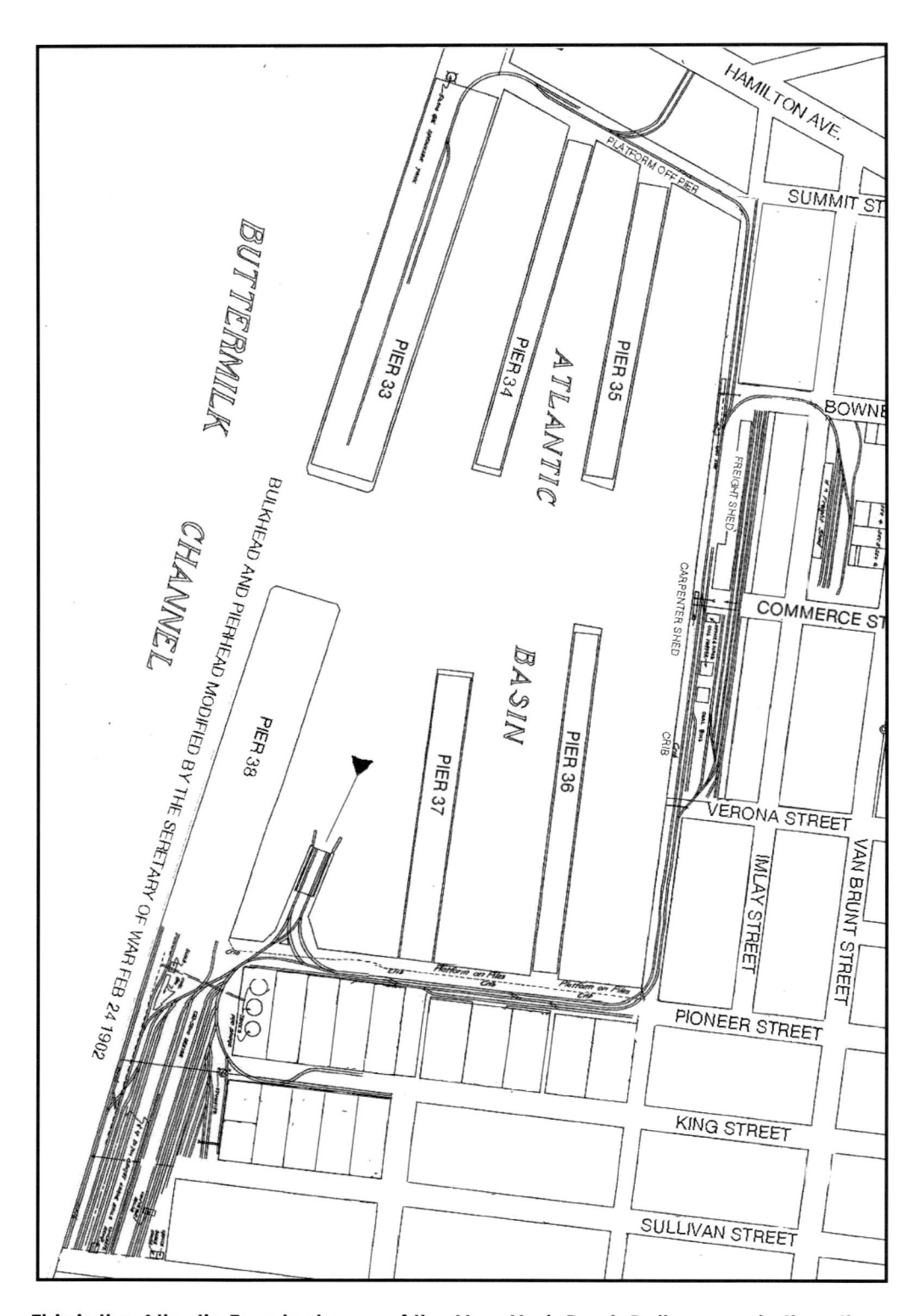

This is the Atlantic Terminal area of the New York Dock Railway; as in the other maps in this volume, the symbol ▼ indicates the location of a car float landing. George Wybenga adapted a rather large track diagram of the New York Dock Railway by J.W. Galbreath dating from 1912 to provide this and the following maps of the New York Dock Railway's three terminals.

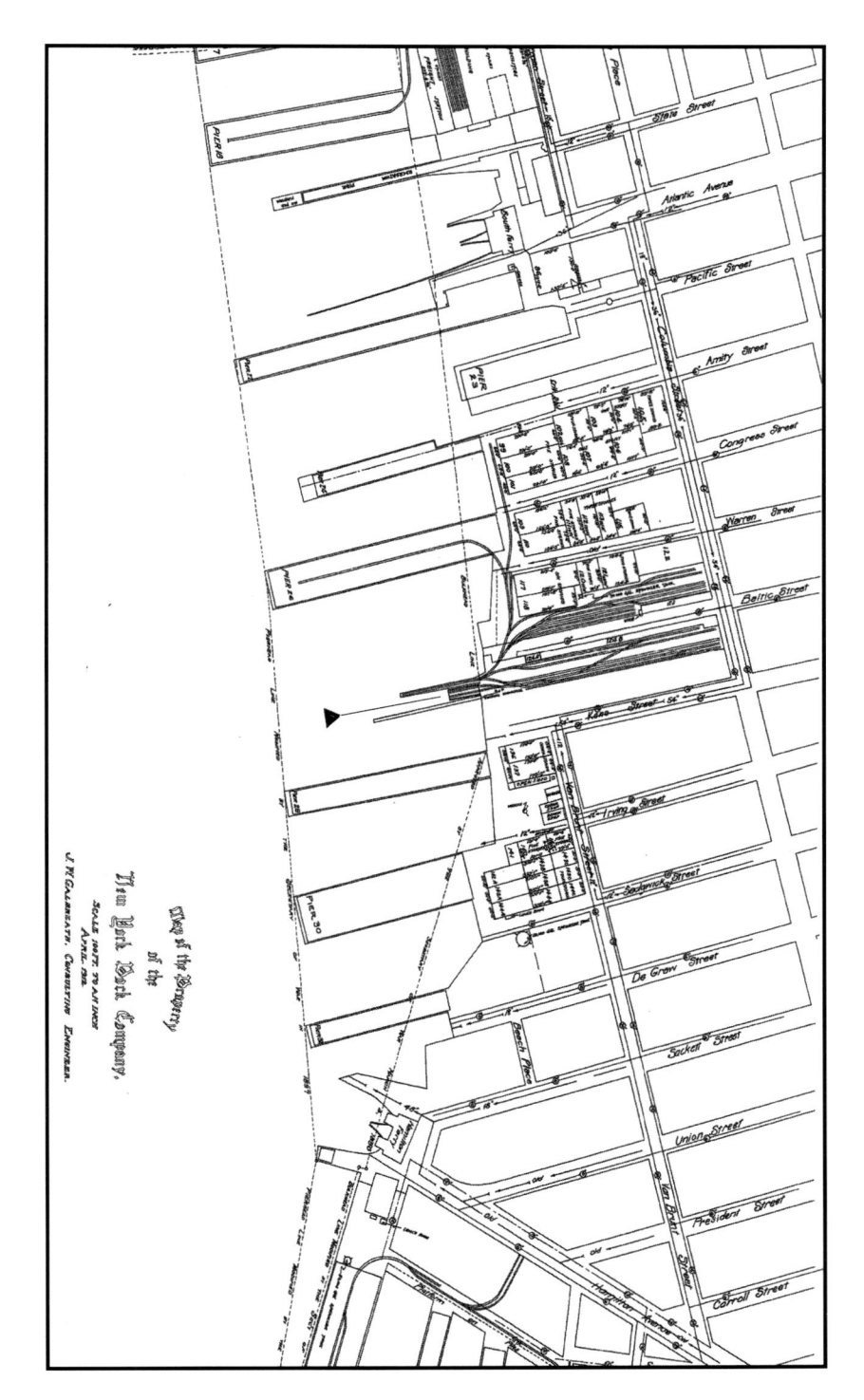

Located in the center of this map is the Baltic Terminal area of the New York Dock Company. This map is to a smaller scale than the other track diagrams primarily to show the relationship of the three New York Dock terminals to each other. The trackage just visible at the top is the southern end of the New York Dock's Fulton Terminal; the trackage at the bottom of the map is the north end of the Atlantic Terminal. From a 1912 diagram of J.W. Galbreath redrawn by George Wybenga.

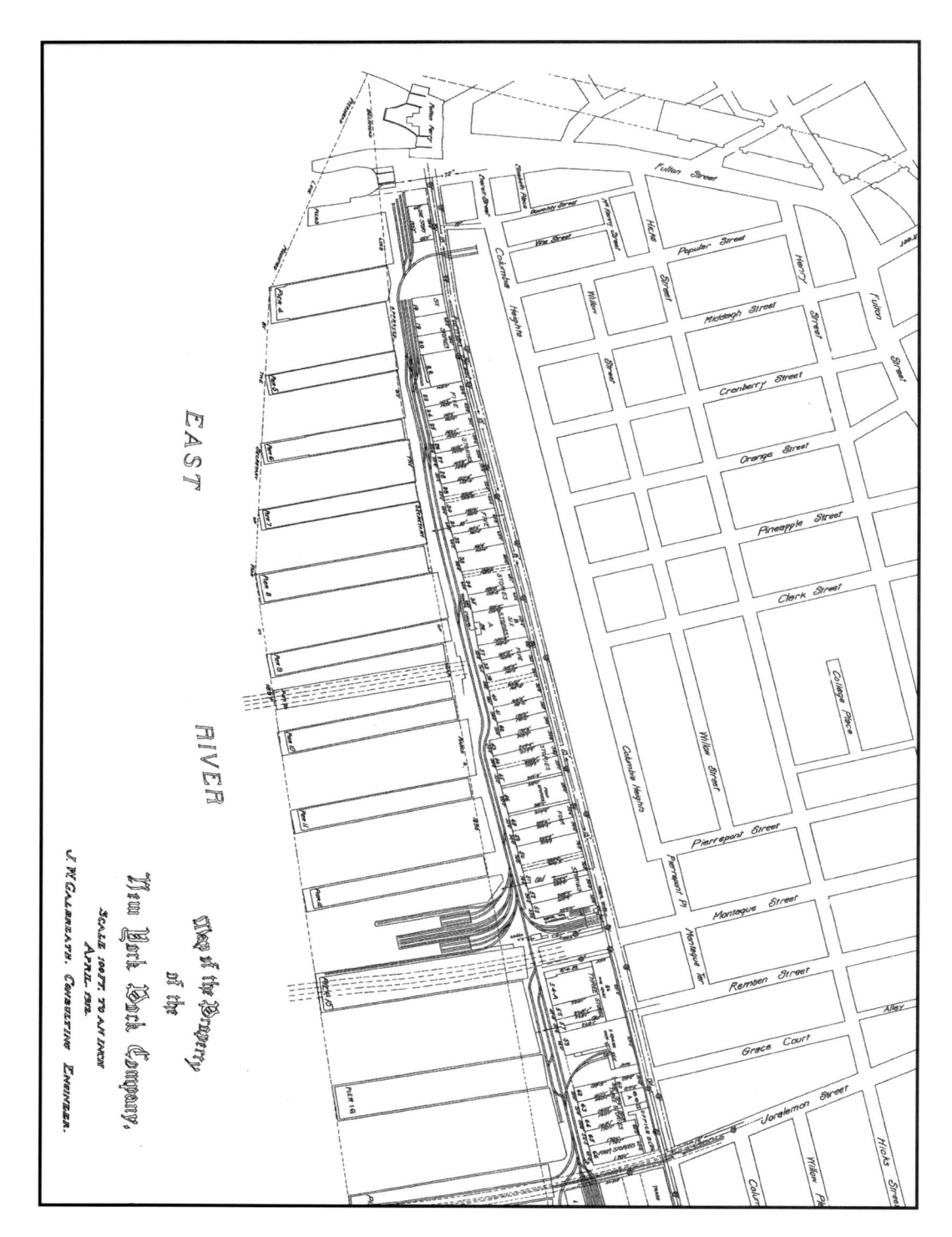

The Fulton Terminal area of the New York Dock Company in another section of the J. W. Galbreath diagram as redrawn by George Wybenga. It should be noted that this area has been extensively changed as a result of the construction of the Brooklyn – Queens Expressway and the Brooklyn Pier Authority's redevelopment project.

DOWN ON THE BROOKLYN DOCKS
NEW YORK DOCK RAILWAY

The history of this enterprise starts with the Brooklyn Wharf and Warehouse Company whose subsidiary; the Brooklyn Wharf Transfer Company began rail operations during 1896 with a four wheel steam dummy type locomotive. By the turn of the century the roster was up to four dummy locomotives and the company had but two months left before slipping into receivership. The February 1900 bankruptcy was resolved through a re-organization.

This builder's photograph of the Brooklyn Wharf and Warehouse Company number 2 raises a few questions; it is known that this locomotive was purchased second hand; usually used locomotives were not lavished with the luxury of a new builder's photograph.

The New York Dock Company was formed on July 18, 1901 and immediately absorbed the remains of the Brooklyn Wharf and Warehouse Company, the Brooklyn Wharf Transfer Company, and the Baltic Realty Company. The rail operations and the rolling stock of the original three companies were now vested in the Railroad Department of the New York Dock Company. At this time the line served as a non-common carrier servicing the docks, warehouses, and freight transfer facilities of its owner.

Under the new ownership the line fared very well, an additional 0.16 mile of track was leased from the Brooklyn Rapid Transit and an electric locomotive constructed by the Baldwin Locomotive Works which was purchased to service consignees along the leased rails. In 1908 the New York Dock Company's brief flirtation with electric operation came to an end with the aptly named *"Brooklyn"* being sold to a shortline railroad in Canada.

The four little dummies were just that, little, which resulted in their gradual supplementation and replacement with five six driver tank engines and an old 'Forney; type rapid transit engine. On April 12, 1910 the New York Dock Railway was incorporated, strangely the Railroad Department assets of its corporate parent was not acquired until October 1, 1912 and then they were only leased! The new entity was intended to be a common carrier terminal switching road.

The 10.91 mile line consisted of three distinct branches or terminals; the Baltic Terminal located at the foot of Columbia and Warren Streets with 2.64 miles of track serving several warehouses and docks. The Fulton Terminal was located beneath the Brooklyn Heights Promenade at Montague and Furman Streets; this was the operating center of the line. The Atlantic Terminal at the Atlantic Basin was the third location, this line served Brooklyn Piers 11 and 12. Interchange between the three

The number 7 simmering in the sun on July 6, 1937.

disconnected segments and the outside world was accomplished through a marine roster of two tugboats and five carfloats.

The first dozen years of the new line were busy; the Interstate Commerce Commission determined that the property was a common carrier engaged in interstate transportation. Four additional steam tank locomotives both the six and four wheel variety were acquired. Yet the road even then was not content to rest upon its motive power laurels as the docks, warehouses, and plants that the New York Dock Railway served were very busy. This resulted in four more tank engines joining the roster in the late Twenties and Thirties; although most of these additional acquisitions were second hand. World War II and the economic upturn to rebuild the nation after the war even pushed the road into Class I status meaning the line had revenues in excess of $1,000,000. The New York Dock Railway was a tidy operation but it was no more a Class I operation than the former Chicago and Northwestern Railway was a terminal railroad around Chicago! The New York Dock Railway did perform a Class I act when they replaced their entire steam locomotive roster in the nine month period between March and December 1951 with the purchase of five General Electric center cab switching locomotives.

The New York Dock Railway's number 41 is seen in this November 19, 1949 view in the Baltic Terminal area. This is the second appearance of this locomotive in this book; it was originally Jay Street Connecting Railroad number 1 and became the property of the New York Dock Railway during 1931.

In the ten years after dieselization the idea of break bulk cargo handling was the normal way that freight was moved through the Port of New York, whether it was via marine, rail, or motor carriage. The idea of long distance container transportation was not foreseen by many in the transportation field, but it was coming. Rising costs saw the New York Dock Railway begin to take some cost savings measures, the general offices located on Whitehall Street in Manhattan were relocated to their station building at Furman and Joralemon Streets in Brooklyn. One of the new locomotives, just five years old was sold to a railway in Cuba. The ultimate cost cutting action was the closing of the small Baltic Terminal and the sale of the property it sat on during 1962. The road was able to keep its operating costs to the level that they had been during 1948 but it was not successful in keeping the operating revenue to a decent level due to changes in the Brooklyn industrial scene and in shipping methods.

The New York Dock Railways history is a fairly straightforward story of cars arriving at the mainline railroads carfloat yard, the green and yellow tugboat and carfloats coming over to get them for the trip across the harbor to Brooklyn where they would be distributed to the factory, warehouse, or pier. Be that the parent company, the New York Dock Company would have had such a simple life also. The New York Dock Company (the real estate firm) was re-organized during 1937 undergoing a major re-capitalization. Then just twenty years later in 1949 the firm sold its real property holdings to the Brooklyn Pier Authority (now a part of the Port Authority of New York and New Jersey) who was intent on redeveloping the Brooklyn waterfront. The timing of this project, 1959, has proven to be most unfortunate. The container revolution in shipping was just on the horizon but the project at hand was to redevelop the Brooklyn area for the traditional break bulk shipping methods. This portion of the Brooklyn waterfront with all of its newly re-developed piers quickly fell into a state of disuse.

THE SHORTLINE RAILROADS OF LONG ISLAND

The lowest number diesel locomotive on the New York Dock Railway was the number 51. Built nominally as a forty-four ton model it was ballasted during construction to a weight of fifty tons. One of three on the roster, it and the 52 remained in service until August 17, 1983. The sister 53 was exported to Cuba in October 1956 becoming the Ferrocarril Consolidados de Cuba (Cubana Railway) in Cuba as their 17.

Meantime back at the rail level, the new parent of the New York Dock Railway was the New York Dock Properties Corporation. The old New York Dock Company was acquired during 1958 by a British based firm, Dunhill International. Dunhill International was a London based holding company that was owned by interests that make and sell the Dunhill brand of cigarettes. The original New York Dock Company had under gone several permutations in name and ownership and is now best recognized as a part of the Questor Toy Company.

Rail service to the Baltic Terminal area ceased during the early 1960's. The New York Dock Properties Company took a positive view of the diminished freight traffic still remaining on the Brooklyn docks and the new ownership began a program of expansion. When the Bush Terminal Railway abandoned their property on December 31, 1972 the New York Dock Railway petitioned the Interstate Commerce Commission to be awarded a directed service order in April 1972 and continued to provide service to the area. The continuance of rail service in the Bush Terminal service area was no doubt a relief to the City of New York who were promoting their 'Industry City' project at the time. As the New York Dock Railway had gone south during April 1972, the line now turned its head north for further expansion and during the winter of 1973 acquired stock control of the Brooklyn Eastern District Terminal. There was no merger intent with the Williamsburg line; both railroads were to operate in a cooperative method side by side. The Brooklyn Eastern District Terminal company's tugboats were repainted into green and yellow and began to be tied up at the Fulton Terminal of the New York Dock Railway.

With these new service areas, the motive power of the New York Dock Railway was expanded. The Bush Terminal's two former military 65 ton switchers were returned to service, they would serve their old territory until March 1980. The two locomotives at Bush Terminal were supplemented with the purchase of two Alco RS-3 type locomotives from the Central of Georgia Railroad which were acquired during 1974. The two large 1600 horsepower locomotives were not a good fit for Bush due to the sharp curves found there, they were supplemented with two General Motors type NW-2 switch

After the New York Dock Railway acquired the three ballasted forty-four ton models they had General Electric build two more similar locomotives. The 54 and the 55 (seen here in an undated image) were fifty ton models which had a larger and heavier frame. The 55 was sold to the Eastern Railcar firm in Hillsdale, New York who resold it to the East Penn Railways Railroad as their 44; it was scrapped on August 13, 2010.

locomotives from the Southern Railway in April 1981 relegating the Alco's to standby service only.

January 1983 was a bad month for the New York Dock Railway. Citing diminished car loadings due to almost all of the freight passing through New York Harbor in containers at the Port Authority of New York and New Jersey's Port Newark and Port Elizabeth container ports; it applied for abandonment of the Fulton Terminal, the Atlantic Terminal, and the Brooklyn Eastern District Terminal. The road was shut down on August 17, 1983 but as so often happens in transportation stories, this abandonment is not the end of the entire story.

- * * * -

THE NEW YORK DOCK RAILWAY AT BUSH TERMINAL

As we noted earlier, on December 31, 1971 the New York Dock Railway petitioned the Interstate Commerce Commission for a directed service order to continue rail service to the Bush Terminal Railway. This document was awarded to the New York Dock Railway in April 1972 and rail service continued to be provided to Bush Terminal. The New York Dock began service using the former Bush Terminal locomotives, particularly the former military 88 and 89 from the Bush Terminal but eventually two Alco road switcher locomotives were acquired from the Southern Railroad family. These two locomotives were not ideal for the confines of Bush Terminal and they were eventually set aside for two Electromotive Division type NW-2 switching locomotives. One of the changes wrought to the Bush Terminal area was an attempt to introduce trailer on flat car ("TOFC") service; this was accompanied by an attempt to set up an interchange with the Penn Central via the Military Ocean Terminal ("MOT") trackage but ultimately both the service and the interchange was shortlived.

The former Bush Terminal 88 re-lettered for the New York Dock Railway switches the main yard at Bush Terminal. This image is from February 12, 1976, and was taken by Matthew J. Herson Jr. and is from the John Scala Collection.

On March 20, 1978 Benjamin W. Schaeffer caught this image of a Conrail freight interchanging with the New York Dock Company on trackage in the Military Ocean Terminal ("MOT"). The locomotive in the distance is Penn Central 9534.

The New York Dock Railway utilized a portable ramp to unload the trailers from the rail cars; usually it was done on the grounds of the Military Ocean Terminal ("MOT") as in this August 1982 image from Benjamin W. Schaeffer.

THE NEW YORK DOCK RAILWAY AT BUSH TERMINAL (continued)

(Right) Coupled to the Bush Terminal's float reach car the former Central of Georgia Railroad (Southern System) 113 as New York Dock Railway 56 posed for the camera of an unknown photographer in May 1974; this image is from the collection of Philip M. Goldstein.

Another view (left) of the 56 standing near the engine house at Bush Terminal; coupled to another engine at the long hood end. This image from the collection of Philip Goldstein was taken by Stan Goldstein on October 11, 1978.

New York Dock Railway 59 (right) rolls down the center of First Avenue with a trailer on flat car ("TOFC") train on March 25, 1983. This image was taken by Benjamin W. Schaeffer. Unfortunately camera technology and quality of 1983 did not match that of today but the rareness of this subject has to be respected.

- * * * -

NEW YORK DOCK RAILWAY

The below engines were the property of the Brooklyn Wharf Transfer Company from the beginning in 1896 until the New York Dock Company was formed on July 18, 1901 after which they were vested in the Railroad Department of the New York Dock Company. On April 12, 1910 the New York Dock Railway was incorporated, and leased the facilities and equipment of the Railroad Department of the New York Dock Company on October 1, 1912.

CLASS	NUMBER	BUILDER	SERIAL	DATE
	first 1	Baldwin Locomotive Works	14969	7/1896

This was a 0-4-0T steam dummy locomotive with compound cylinders, one was 10x17, the other 10x24, with 44 inch drivers built for the Brooklyn Wharf Transfer Company as their first number 1; apparently out of service circa 1916; sold to the Richards and Gaston for use at their Hillside Quarry in Lakewood, New Jersey in May 1922 as their 5. No further information.

| | second 1 | PW&B RR – Wilmington | none | __/1889 |

This was a used 0-4-0 that had been built in the Wilmington Shops of the Philadelphia, Wilmington, and Baltimore Railroad with 15x24 cylinders and an unknown driver diameter as their 572 becoming Pennsylvania Railroad third 572 at a later date. This locomotive was sold to the Southern Iron and Equipment Company in October 9, 1914 receiving their number 978. The New York Dock Railway purchased this locomotive as their second number 1 on March 13, 1916. No retirement data is known.

| | 2 | Baldwin Locomotive Works | 14970 | 7/1896 |

This was a used 0-4-0T dummy steam locomotive with compound cylinders, one 10x17 and the other 10x24 with a driver diameter of 44 inches. This locomotive was acquired by the Brooklyn Wharf Transfer Company on an unknown date from Richards and Gaston who in turn had obtained it from Calco Chemicals. This locomotive remained in service as New York Dock Railway 2 only until May 1919 when it was sold.

| | 3 | Baldwin Locomotive Works | 15288 | 4/1897 |

This was a 0-4-0T dummy steam locomotive with 17x24 cylinders and a 44 inch driver diameter, purchased as Brooklyn Wharf Transfer 3. This locomotive was sold in November 1930 to the William Mosser Company.

The crewman working with the 27 appears to be closely monitoring its progress across a certain section of trackage in this August 3, 1938 image. That date creates a problem because according to the records the 27 wasn't acquired until April 4, 1942; perhaps this action occurred in 1948?

New York Dock 34 in a moment of repose in an undated image from the Fagerberg collection. The 34 was built as National Slag Company 1 named "*America*" and was converted to oil burning during 1931. This locomotive was acquired on an unknown date as New York Dock Railway 34; it was retired during 1951.

NEW YORK DOCK RAILWAY (continued)

CLASS	NUMBER	BUILDER	SERIAL	DATE
	4	Baldwin Locomotive Works	16031	7/1898

This was a 0-4-0T dummy steam tank locomotive with 17x24 cylinders and a 44 inch driver diameter, purchased as Brooklyn Wharf Transfer 4. This locomotive was scrapped during 1932.

| | 5 | Pittsburgh Locomotive Co | 1515 | 1/1894 |

This was a 0-4-4T 'Forney' style rapid transit tank steam locomotive with 12x16 cylinders and 42 inch drivers that was delivered as Manhattan Elevated 201. This locomotive was acquired in November 1905 by the Railroad Department of the New York Dock Company and was renumbered to 5; it was sold on January 6, 1906 to the Day Lumber and Manufacturing Company in Richardson, Mississippi.

	6	Baldwin Locomotive Works	31607	8/1907
	7	Baldwin Locomotive Works	31983	10/1907
	8	Baldwin Locomotive Works	32613	1/1908

These were three 0-6-0T steam tank locomotives with 17x24 cylinders and 44 inch diameter drivers as the Railroad Department of the New York Dock Company numbers 6 to 8. All three of these locomotives were converted to oil firing during 1931. The 6 was scrapped during 1932, there is no retirement data for the 7 or 8.

| | 9 | H.K. Porter Co. | 4564 | 4/1910 |

This was a 0-6-0T steam tank locomotive with 17x24 cylinders and an unknown driver diameter, built as the Railroad Department of the New York Dock Company's 9. There is no retirement data for this locomotive.

| | 10 | Alco | 59089 | 1/1918 |
| | 11 | Alco | 59090 | 1/1918 |

These were two 0-4-0T steam tank locomotives of unknown dimensions that were built by an unknown works of the American Locomotive Company ("ALCO"); it is thought that the 10 was scrapped circa 1933, there is no retirement data for the 11. Not all sources agree on the existence of these two locomotives. Similarly, there is a mention of a locomotive 12 but there is no data available for it.

| | 22 | Baldwin Locomotive Works | 14605 | __/1895 |

This was a 0-4-0T steam tank locomotive of unknown dimensions that is believed to have been built for the Carnegie Street Company in Pittsburgh, Pennsylvania, subsequently sold to the Union Railroad. This locomotive was rebuilt by the Alco – Cooke Works during July 1913; it was subsequently purchased by the New York Dock Railway as their 22; it was sold circa 1940 to a cement company located in Castleton on the Hudson, New York.

| | 27 | Baldwin Locomotive Works | 41630 | 8/1914 |

This was a 0-6-0T steam tank locomotive with 20x26 cylinders and 50 inch diameter drivers that was built as Philadelphia Slag Company 2 but was delivered to the National Slag Company in South Bethlehem, Pennsylvania as their number 2. Converted by the Baldwin Locomotive Works to burn oil circa 1932 and purchased by the New York Dock Company as their 27 on April 4, 1942. This locomotive was retired during 1951.

| | 34 | Baldwin Locomotive Works | 45354 | 3/1917 |

This was a 0-6-0T steam locomotive, the dimensions might have been 20x26 cylinders and 50 inch drivers; it was built as National Slag Company 1 named "*America*" and was converted to oil burning during 1931. This locomotive was acquired on an unknown date as New York Dock Railway 34; it was retired during 1951.

THE SHORTLINE RAILROADS OF LONG ISLAND

NEW YORK DOCK RAILWAY (continued)

CLASS	NUMBER	BUILDER	SERIAL	DATE
	36	H.K. Porter Co	5568	5/1914

This was a 0-6-0T steam tank locomotive with 18x24 cylinders with unknown diameter drivers built as Watertown Arsenal, Massachusetts number 11 later passing to the Aluminum Corporation of American ("Alcoa") in Massena, New York as their 11; it was probably on the roster of the Massena Terminal Company (an Alcoa subsidiary) as their 11 for a time. This locomotive was converted to oil burning during 1931 and was acquired by the New York Dock Company in April 1942; scrapped during 1951.

| | 40 | Alco – Cooke Works | 62761 | 7/1921 |

This was a 0-6-0T steam tank locomotive built by the American Locomotive Company ("Alco") at their Cooke Works with 16x24 cylinders and 42 inch diameter drivers that was built for the Fleischmann's Yeast Company of Peekskill, New York as their 1. This locomotive was acquired on an unknown date as New York Dock Railway 40, it was scrapped during 1948.

| | 41 | Baldwin Locomotive Works | 27255 | 1/1906 |

This is a 0-6-0ST side tank steam locomotive with 19x24 cylinders and 46 inch diameter drivers delivered new as Jay Street Terminal Railroad 1, to Jay Street Connecting Railroad 1 through a re-incorporation of the property on October 9, 1909. The 1 was stored during 1930; it was sold during 1931 to the New York Dock Company as their 41, which was scrapped during 1951.

| | 46 | H.K. Porter Co | 7099 | 5/1928 |

This was a 0-6-0 steam tank locomotive with 18x24 cylinders and an unknown driver diameter that was built for the Wagner Quarries in Sandusky, Ohio as their 99 "*Sunny Sparrow*", acquired by the New York Dock Company on an unknown date as their 46. This locomotive was retired during 1951.

Seen here working in an October 10, 1948 image at Atlantic Terminal is number 36. This locomotive began its history with the U.S. Army at the Watertown Arsenal in Massachusetts and had an interim owner before reaching Brooklyn.

Looking forlorn as it stands in this October 19, 1948 image is New York Dock number 40; it was due to be retired that same year. The building in the background suggests that this is the Baltic Terminal.

| | 47 | Alco – Schenectady Works | 62502 | 8/1920 |

This was a 0-6-0T steam tank locomotive built by the American Locomotive Company ("Alco") at their Schenectady Works with 21x26 cylinders and 50 inch diameter drivers built as Standard Oil Company 5 for use in Baton Rouge, Louisiana. This locomotive was acquired on an unknown date by the New York Dock Railway as their 47. This locomotive was retired during 1951.

NEW YORK DOCK RAILWAY (continued)

CLASS	NUMBER	BUILDER	SERIAL	DATE
	48	Alco – Schenectady Works	65982	11/1924

This was a 0-6-0T steam tank locomotive built by the American Locomotive Company ("Alco") at their Schenectady Works with 21x26 cylinders with 50 inch diameter drivers built as Vacuum Oil 4 and was then Standard Oil Company 7 for use in Baton Rouge, Louisiana. This locomotive was acquired on an unknown date by the New York Dock Railway as their 48. This locomotive was retired during 1951.

The number 47 began life working at a refinery in Louisiana before coming north to the New York Dock Company. The locomotive is on the Fulton Terminal float bridge and posed on September 9, 1949.

The fifty ton number 54 pauses outside of the office of the Monti Marine Corporation in the Atlantic Terminal in this undated image from the Fagerberg collection.

| | 51 to 53 | General Electric | 30581 to 30583 | 3/1951 |

These are three B-B trucked 44 ton model diesel electric locomotives that were ballasted to a weight of fifty tons. The 51 and 52 remained in service until August 17, 1983 after which they were stored on a barge at the Fulton Terminal until 1986 when they were transported to New Jersey for scrapping. Locomotive 53 was sold in October 1956 to the Ferrocarril Consolidados de Cuba (Cubana Railway) in Cuba as their 17; this locomotive was not renumbered into the 'All Cuba; numbering system and was last seen out of service during the early 1980's.

| | 54 to 55 | General Electric | 31224 to 31225 | 12/1951 |

These are two B-B trucked 50 ton model diesel electric locomotives that differed from the 44 ton model by having a different and deeper frame. Both of these locomotives were taken out of service on August 17, 1983 and stored on a barge at the Fulton Terminal. The 54 was transported to New Jersey during 1986 where it was scrapped. The 55 was sold to the Eastern Railcar firm in Hillsdale, New York who resold it to the East Penn Railways as their 44; it was scrapped August 13, 2010.

The fifty ton number 55 presents a dramatic view in this undated end on image.

THE SHORTLINE RAILROADS OF LONG ISLAND PAGE 59

NEW YORK DOCK RAILWAY (continued)

CLASS	NUMBER	BUILDER	SERIAL	DATE
	56	Alco	78756	5/1951
	57	Alco	78755	5/1951

These were two American Locomotive Company ("Alco") RS-3 model 1600 horsepower road switchers built for the Central of Georgia Railroad (Southern System) as their 114 and 113; they were sold to the New York Dock Railway in April 1974 for use at the former Bush Terminal Railway location. These two locomotives were stored out of service during 1981 and after August 17, 1983 they were stored on a barge at the Fulton Terminal. The 56 and 57 were transported to New Jersey during 1986 where they were scrapped.

New York Dock's 56 was photographed on April 20, 1979 by Benjamin W. Schaeffer stored between a former Brooklyn Eastern District Terminal S1 and a former Bush Terminal Railway 65 ton switcher.

The 57 standing in Bush Terminal in Bush Terminal on October 22, 1974 in an image by the late Gerald Landau from the collection of Philip M. Goldstein.

	58	Electromotive Division	3645	5/1951
	59	Electromotive Division	4753	11/1947

These were two Electomotive Division, General Motors Corporation model NW-2 end cab switch locomotives that had been built as Southern Railway 2234 and 2253, being numbered to 1026 and 1044 in November1972. These two locomotives were acquired during April 1981 as New York Dock Railway 58 and 59 to replace two larger locomotives at Bush Terminal. These two locomotives were retired on August 17, 1983 but were acquired by the New York Cross Harbor as their 58 and 59 in August 1983. The 58 was sold for scrap in July 2006; the 59 was sold during 2001 to Cleaner Earth Remediation in Jersey City, New Jersey where it remains stored.

The 58 switching in Bush Terminal on October 28, 1982 in an image by Frank Szachacz from the Philip M. Goldstein collection.

Benjamin W. Schaeffer caught this image of the 59 in the Bush Terminal yard on January 21, 1983.

NEW YORK DOCK RAILWAY (continued)

CLASS	NUMBER	BUILDER	SERIAL	DATE
	Bush 88	**General Electric**	**18014**	**7/1943**

This was a B-B trucked center cab 400 horsepower diesel locomotive that had been built as United States Army Transportation Corps 7864. Acquired by the Bush Terminal Company during 1956; transferred to the New York Dock Railway in January 1974 and scrapped in March 1980.

	Bush 89	**General Electric**	**28241**	**9/1945**

This was a B-B trucked center cab 400 horsepower diesel locomotive that had been built for the United States Marine Corps, its road number unknown. Acquired by the Bush Terminal Company during 1962; transferred to the New York Dock Railway in January 1974 and scrapped in March 1980.

	"Brooklyn" [1]	**Baldwin Locomotive Works**	**21488**	**1/1903**

This was a B-B trucked steeple cab 25 ton electric locomotive that was built for the Railroad Department of the New York Dock Company. *"Brooklyn"* was used on the electrified trackage leased from the Brooklyn Rapid Transit. This locomotive was sold in December 1908 to the Chatham, Wallaceburg and Lake Erie Railway in Canada, as their 20, further resold during 1928 to the Cornwall Street Railway as their first number 11; this locomotive was scrapped during 1950.

This image is undated, the focus and lighting are not the best, but it is a wonderfully atmospheric view of the Fulton Terminal float bridge area. Try dating it yourself; all of the freight cars appear to be of wood construction.

- * * * -

---

[1] One source states that this locomotive may have carried the number 5 but that would conflict with the use of this number on the former Manhattan Elevated Railway 'Forney' locomotive.

MISS PHOEBE SNOW OF BROOKLYN, NEW YORK

BROOKLYN DOCK AND TERMINAL RAILWAY
DELAWARE, LACKAWANNA AND WESTERN RAILROAD

- * * * -

DL&W 25th STREET YARD

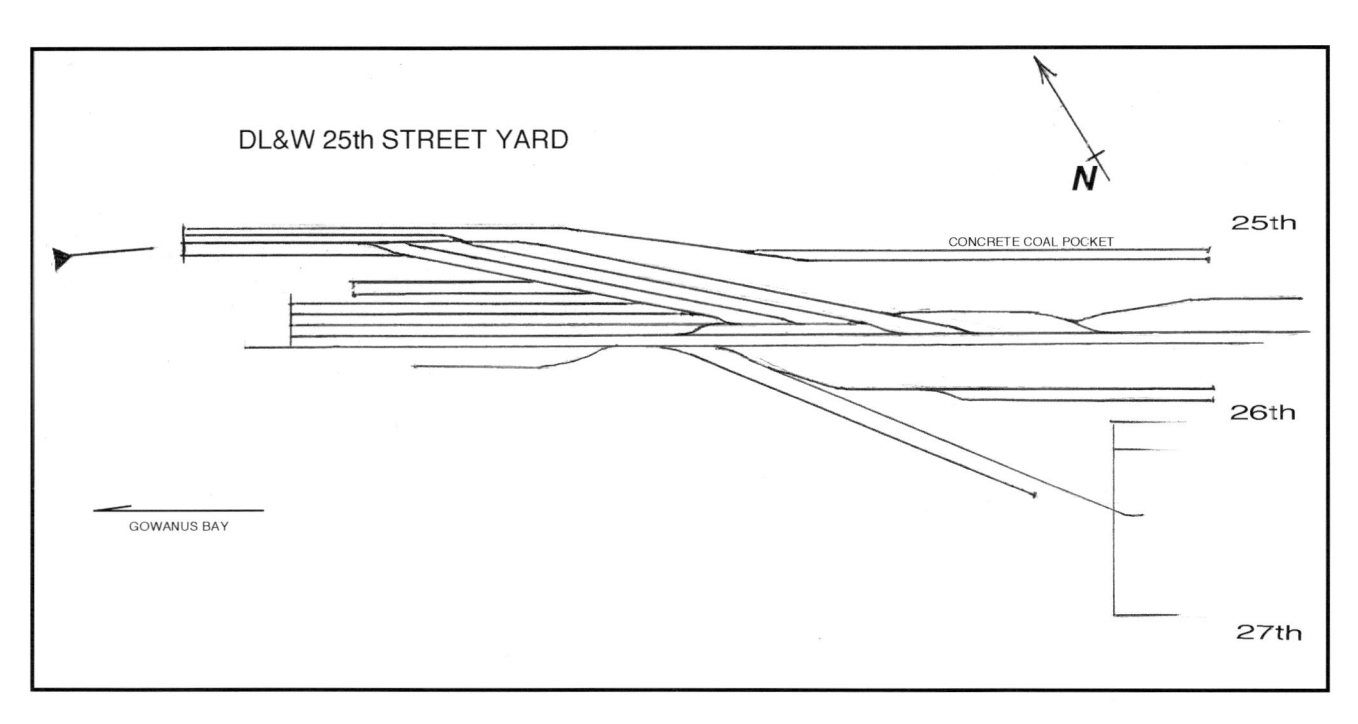

CONCRETE COAL POCKET

25th

26th

27th

GOWANUS BAY

N

The 25th Street facility was located just north of the Bush Terminal area on the southern boundary of Sunset Park. If you look on the Bush Terminal track diagram shown on page 30 this yard is partially cutoff at the bottom of that image. This is a George Wybenga image based on a Delaware, Lackawanna and Western Railway diagram of the facility.

MISS PHOEBE SNOW OF BROOKLYN, NEW YORK
BROOKLYN DOCK AND TERMINAL RAILWAY
DELAWARE, LACKAWANNA AND WESTERN RAILROAD

Brooklyn Dock and Terminal Railway

On May 1, 1899 five individuals met to incorporate the Brooklyn Dock and Terminal Railway. The group consisted of Daniel A. Heald of Orange, New Jersey, Robert B Roosevelt and J.B. Van Wert, both of New York, New York, Cornelius P. Blauvelt of Nyack, New York, and Commodore P. Vedder whose full address is given as 136 Liberty Street, New York, New York. Each of these gentlemen held ten shares of stock of the new corporation.

The company was formed to provide a union terminal next to the site of the former Erie Canal Terminal at the foot of Twenty-Fifth Street in Brooklyn. These premises were located mainly on a pier that extended into Gowanus Bay. For motive power, a small six driver tank engine was purchased from the Norfolk and Western Railway. The line had no physical connection with any other railroad in the New York Harbor area, and no apparent corporate connection with any other line, this being part of the source of the 'union terminal'; identification of the operation.

Among the documents preserved by the Clerk of the County of New York are the annual reports of the Brooklyn Dock and Terminal Railway for their first three years. Unlike their modern counterparts, the information contained in these documents is extremely sparse, to wit:

Year Ending	January 23, 1900	January 22, 1901	January 21, 1902
Value of Assets	$67,000	$80,000	$90,000
Outstanding Debts	$90,000	$80,000	$90,000
Par Value of Stock	$1,500,000	$1,500,000	$1,500,000

The reports are completely silent as to matters of income and expenses and are financially indecipherable!

A builders photograph of the Brooklyn Dock and Terminal's number 2; it would later become Delaware, Lackawanna and Western first 173.

Business however was good enough for the line to purchase an additional locomotive, a six driver saddle tanker numbered 2 was delivered in March 1904 by the Baldwin Locomotive Works.

The little road lost its' union terminal image on December 26, 1906 when the shareholders sold all of the assets to the Delaware, Lackawanna and Western Railroad. The Brooklyn Dock and Terminal Railway Corporation was dissolved as of December 26, 1906.

- * * * -

Delaware, Lackawanna and Western Railroad

The new owners of the little property quickly brought the premises at the foot of Twenty-Fifth Street under their banner, even though their only physical connection with the line was via a carfloat. Of the two locomotives that the Brooklyn Dock and Terminal had rostered, only the number 2, which had been purchased new survived into the new regime. It quickly became Delaware, Lackawanna and Western Railroad 173, later renumbered 8. The City of New York banned the use of coal fired steam locomotives on lines within the municipal boundaries and this resulted in the retirement of the little tank engine during 1926. The replacement motive power was one of the earliest installations of a diesel locomotive in the United States. DL&W 3001, a six hundred horsepower boxcab locomotive was built by a consortium of the American Locomotive Company ("Alco"), General Electric, and Ingersoll-Rand, was unloaded from the float bridge to take up residence in Brooklyn during June 1926.

The Twenty-Fifth Street facility was completely rebuilt during 1929 with a ramp to unload automobiles from boxcars and a coal trestle for hopper cars. The yard continued in service for a number of years, the old boxcab giving way to a General Electric forty-four ton model diesel locomotive after World War II, but the car loadings were diminishing. By the time of the October 17, 1960 merger of the Erie with the Delaware, Lackawanna and Western, this facility was declining in use and was subsequently closed circa 1964.

- * * * -

The Lackawanna had an additional operation physically located on Long Island besides the Gowanus Bay location at the foot of Twenty-Fifth Street. Shortly after the start of the Twentieth Century, the Delaware, Lackawanna and Western Railroad acquired a portion of the waterfront along the Wallabout Basin area of Brooklyn. Additional land was created by filling out the property to the bulkhead line and a rail yard was built on it. Like the former Brooklyn Dock and Terminal property, the only physical connection with the mainline on the mainland was via a carfloat.

There were no photographs of any Lackawanna diesels on Long Island in the Fagerberg collection, but there were several images taken on the Harlem Transfer up in the Bronx, these included Harlem Transfer number 53 which as Lackawanna third 53 had been the assigned motive power at 25th Street.

For motive power in the Wallabout Basin yard, a four wheel tank engine that had been built in the shops of the Utica, Chenango and Susquehanna Valley before that upstate line was merged into the Lackawanna, was floated across the harbor. This locomotive, when it needed servicing, was sent over to the Jersey City roundhouse which then sent a relief engine to cover the Wallabout Basin. Just as the New York City ordinances had forced the steam locomotive off of the Gowanus Bay property, the same occurred here. The replacement at this location was not an early diesel but a double truck electric locomotive that resulted in this yard being equipped with a 600 volt direct current catenary.

Delaware, Lackawanna and Western Railroad (continued)

The start of World War II saw a buildup and expansion at the Brooklyn Navy Yard and this resulted in the Delaware, Lackawanna and Western's property being condemned for shipyard expansion in late 1941. The little fifty ton electric locomotive was sold to a shortline in Canada for further service. The Lackawanna freight consignees who remained in Brooklyn were undoubtedly served from the former Brooklyn Dock and Terminal property until its closure about 1960.

- * * * -

Both of these locations were linked to their parent's mainline facilities through the use of floating or marine equipment. What is perhaps one of the best discussions of railway marine equipment in the present author's opinion can be found in the book Taber, Thomas Townsend (deceased) and Taber, Thomas Townsend, III: **THE DELAWARE, LACKAWANNA & WESTERN IN THE TWENTIETH CENTURY – VOLUME II – Equipment and Marine**; published by Thomas Townsend Taber III; Muncy, Pennsylvania, 1981.

The late Frank Zahn captured this image of the Lackawanna's 4001 working in the Wallabout Basin Terminal. Image from the collection of Edward M. Koehler Jr.

- * * * -

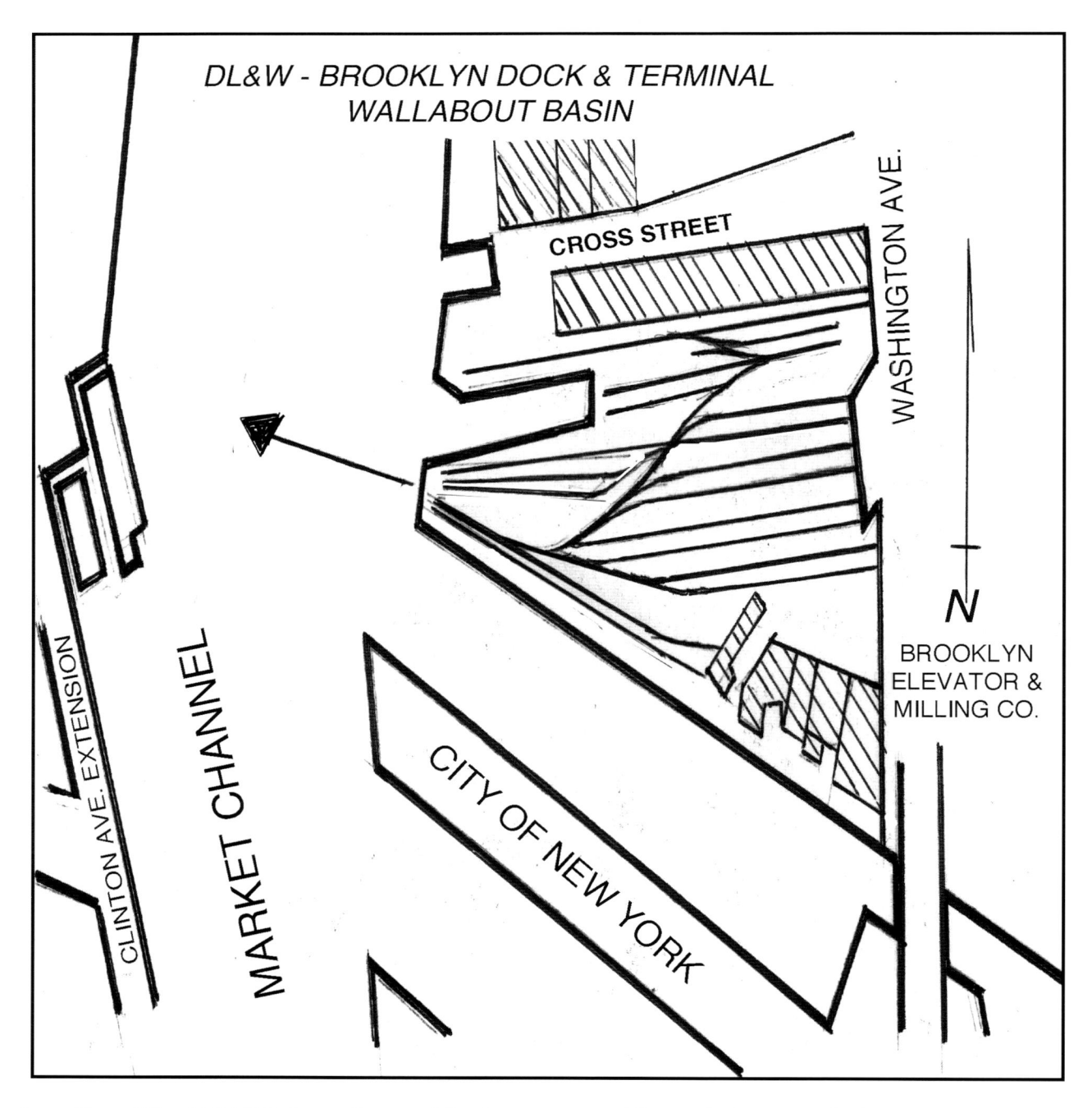

A section of the 1924 U.S. Army Corps of Engineers map of the Port of New York that shows the Wallabout Basin in Brooklyn that has been extensively redrawn by George Wybenga. Don't bother looking on a modern map for this location; the U.S. Navy annexed the west shore of the Wallabout Basin in late 1941 adding it to the Brooklyn Navy Yard. The area has been extensively rebuilt. The original map image was contributed by James Guthrie.

BROOKLYN DOCK AND TERMINAL RAILWAY

CLASS	NUMBER	BUILDER	SERIAL	DATE
	1	Baldwin	6705	4/1883

This was a 0-6-2T steam tank locomotive with 17x24 cylinders and 49 inch diameter drivers that was built as Norfolk and Western Railway first Class A first 93; this locomotive was sold to the Brooklyn Dock and Terminal Railway in July 1899. This locomotive was apparently retired circa 1906 as it was not taken over in the Delaware, Lackawanna and Western Railroad in their December 26, 1906 purchase of the Brooklyn Dock and Terminal Railway. No further information.

| | 2 | Baldwin | 23868 | 3/1904 |

This was a 0-6-0 steam tank locomotive with 19x24 cylinders and 46½ inch diameter drivers that was built new for the Brooklyn Dock and Terminal Railway. This locomotive was acquired by the Delaware, Lackawanna and Western Railroad in their December 26, 1906 purchase of the Brooklyn Dock and Terminal Railway becoming their first 173. This locomotive was renumbered to fourth 8 during 1914 and scrapped during 1926.

- * * * -

DELAWARE, LACKAWANNA AND WESTERN RAILROAD

This roster is limited to those locomotives known to have served in Brooklyn in terms of steam locomotives and those permanently assigned to Brooklyn for the diesel locomotives. Those desiring full information on the Lackawanna's locomotive roster are recommended to the Taber books shown in the bibliography.

CLASS	NUMBER	BUILDER	SERIAL	DATE
	first 1	UC&SV Utica Shops	none	__/1881

This was a 0-4-0 steam tank locomotive with 15x22 cylinders and 48 inch diameter drivers was the second built in the Utica Shops of the Utica, Chenango and Susquehanna Valley, it was numbered UC&SV second 9 when built and became Delaware, Lackawanna and Western Railroad first 1 through an 1899 merger and system renumbering. This locomotive was transferred to the Wallabout Basin facility at its opening, remaining there until it was retired during 1926.

| | third 4 | Alco – Rogers Works | 53119 | __/1913 |

This was a 0-4-0 steam tank locomotive with 16x24 cylinders and 46 inch diameter drivers that was acquired new for use as a shop engine at the Jersey City roundhouse; it was also used for relief purposes at the Wallabout Basin property, this locomotive was not seen after the electrification of the yard. This locomotive was sold to the Georgia Car and Locomotive Company, an equipment dealer in March 1942; no further information.

| | fourth 8 | Baldwin | 23868 | 3/1904 |

This was a 0-6-0 steam tank locomotive with 19x24 cylinders and 46½ inch diameter drivers that was built new for the Brooklyn Dock and Terminal Railway. This locomotive was acquired by the Delaware, Lackawanna and Western Railroad in their December 26, 1906 purchase of the Brooklyn Dock and Terminal Railway becoming their first 173. This locomotive was renumbered to fourth 8 during 1914 and scrapped during 1926.

DELAWARE, LACKAWANNA AND WESTERN RAILROAD (continued)

CLASS	NUMBER	BUILDER	SERIAL	DATE
	third 53	**General Electric**	**29988**	**11/1948**

This was a 400 horsepower B-B trucked forty-four ton model diesel locomotive which was used to replace the 3001 at the former Brooklyn Dock and Terminal Railway property[1]. This locomotive passed to the Erie-Lackawanna as their 53 as a result of an October 17, 1960 merger. This locomotive was transferred to Harlem Transfer Railway (an Erie-Lackawanna subsidiary line) in the Bronx as their 53 during 1963. The third 53 was sold to the Weston and Brooker Sand and Gravel Company as their 53, passing to Martin Marietta Aggregates as their 18562 on an unknown date, to Martin Marietta 14 by October 1974 for use in Warrenton, Georgia.

| | **first 173** | **Baldwin** | **23868** | **3/1904** |

This was a 0-6-0 steam tank locomotive with 19x24 cylinders and 46½ inch diameter drivers that was built new for the Brooklyn Dock and Terminal Railway. This locomotive was acquired by the Delaware, Lackawanna and Western Railroad in their December 26, 1906 purchase of the Brooklyn Dock and Terminal Railway becoming their first 173. This locomotive was renumbered to fourth 8 during 1914 and scrapped during 1926.

Before the 3001 arrived in Brooklyn to take up its duties, the General Electric Company and the Lackawanna posed it for some publicity photographs. This picture dates from 1926 and the actual location is unknown.

| | **3001** | **Alco – GE – IR** | **66683** | **6/1926** |

This was a 600 horsepower B-B trucked boxcab diesel electric locomotive that was built by a consortium of the <u>A</u>merican <u>L</u>ocomotive <u>Co</u>mpany ("Alco"), <u>G</u>eneral <u>E</u>lectric ("GE"), and <u>I</u>ngersoll-<u>R</u>and ("IR"). The General Electric Company assigned builders number 10026 to this unit (the Alco one is shown above). The 3001 was sold in July 1951 to Ingersoll Rand for use as a plant switcher in Philipsburg, New Jersey. This locomotive was retired by Ingersoll Rand and acquired by the Illinois Railroad Museum of Union, Illinois for preservation in August 1984.

| | **4001** | **General Electric** | **10046** | **6/1926** |

This was a B-B trucked steeple cab electric locomotive acquired new for use at the electrified Wallabout Basin property replacing steam locomotive first 1. This locomotive was removed from service when the yard property was taken over by the United States Navy. This locomotive was sold February 28, 1942 to the Shawinigan Falls Terminal Railway in Canada as their 7; it is believed that this locomotive was scrapped during 1952.

- * * * -

---

[1] There is photographic evidence that a General Electric forty-four ton model (DL&W third 51) and an early Alco diesel switch locomotive (DL&W 401, a model HH600); may have relieved the third 53 at the Twenty-Fifth Street yard at different times.

MAINLAND MAINLINE – ISLAND SHORTLINE

The

**BALTIMORE AND OHIO RAILROAD
CENTRAL RAILROAD OF NEW JERSEY – ERIE RAILROAD
LEHIGH VALLEY RAILROAD – NEW YORK CENTRAL SYSTEM
NEW YORK, NEW HAVEN AND HARTFORD RAILROAD
PENNSYLVANIA RAILROAD**

on Long Island

- * * * -

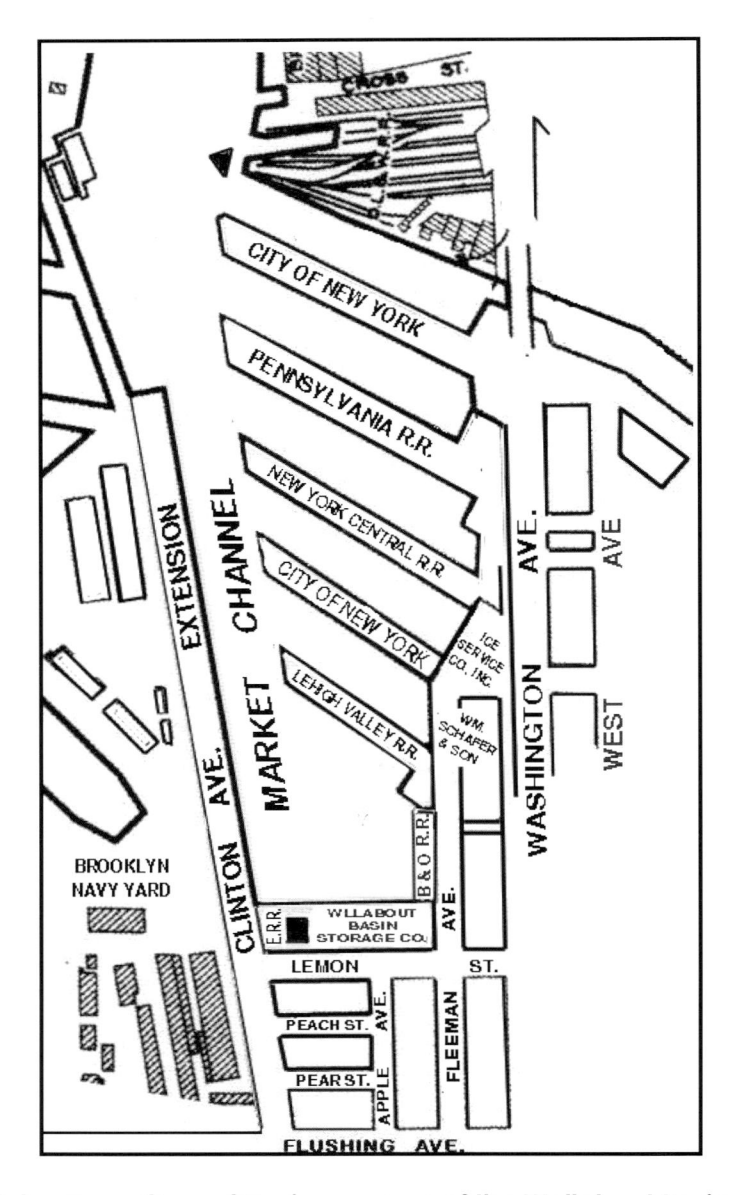

A United States Army Corp of Engineers map of the Wallabout Basin area circa 1924; courtesy of James Guthrie which has been redrawn by George Wybenga for clarity. The piers of the New York Central System, the Lehigh Valley Railroad, and the Baltimore and Ohio Railroad can be clearly seen. The legend "E.R.R.", by the black square (■) in the lower center marks the location the Erie Railroad's freight house on the Wallabout Basin. The Brooklyn Dock and Terminal (Delaware, Lackawanna and Western) is at the top of this image, south of Cross Street. Twelve years after the approximate date of this map the City of New York's Wallabout Market was built in the area bounded by the Clinton Avenue Extension, Lemon Street, Fleeman Avenue, and Flushing Avenue. The market was opened on May 3, 1936 with the Brooklyn Eastern District Terminal being granted exclusive rail access to this location. After the start of World War II in 1941 this entire area was annexed to the Brooklyn Navy Yard (on the left side of this image) and was totally redeveloped.

MAINLAND MAINLINE – ISLAND SHORTLINE
Baltimore and Ohio Railroad – Central Railroad of New Jersey – Erie Railroad
Lehigh Valley Railroad – New York Central System
New York, New Haven and Hartford Railroad – Pennsylvania Railroad

Besides the terminal roads that serviced the East River piers along the Brooklyn and Queens waterfront, five of the nation's major railroads also maintained terminals on Long Island. The story of the Delaware, Lackawanna and Western Railroad in Brooklyn had been documented elsewhere, but that leaves us with a few additional operations. With one exception all of these locations did not have a physical connection to the rest of the nation's rail system; they were linked entirely by the use of marine equipment[1]. In researching the rail terminals of Long Island it is important to note that some of the terminal railways that we are familiar with signed agency agreements with many of the mainline railroads in the early years of the Twentieth Century.

Wallabout Basin

The Wallabout Basin as it has been termed, was located just south of the Wallabout Basin facility of the Delaware, Lackawanna and Western Railroad. This location consisted of five piers and a facility located along a bulkhead. The Pennsylvania Railroad, the New York Central System, and the Lehigh Valley Railroad occupied three of the piers; the City of New York leased the other two piers. The Baltimore and Ohio Railroad was the occupant of a bulkhead structure along what was then Freeman Avenue. It appears that construction of this facility began after November 1, 1898 and the Pennsylvania Railroad had their pier in service prior to June 1, 1900. The Lehigh Valley, New York Central System, and the Central Railroad of New Jersey appear to have been asked to join the Pennsylvania Railroad here circa 1906; the Jersey Central appears to have stayed here only until 1913[2]. This author has only been able to locate a good history of one of the roads who maintained a terminal here, I will share it.

The 'Route of the Black Diamond', the Lehigh Valley Railroad operated a mainline that stretched from Jersey City, New Jersey to Buffalo, New York via Bethlehem and Wilkes-Barre in Pennsylvania and Geneva in New York. This railroad established a freight terminal on the Hudson River in the Greenville section of Jersey City with the National Docks Company as a terminal agent. A yard was constructed in Manhattan at West 27th Street. Several storefront delivery offices were also opened in Manhattan. Also opened were six pier head style terminals, five of them were on the island of Manhattan and outside the scope of our story. The sixth pier terminal of the Lehigh Valley was opened during 1906 adjacent to the Delaware, Lackawanna, and Western's former Brooklyn Dock and Terminal facility in Wallabout Basin. To service this facility, modified carfloats known as 'station floats' were utilized. The usual carfloat in New York Harbor was a three track affair which narrowed to two at one end. In the station float variant the center track is not present being replaced by a raised platform that is at the floor level of a boxcar. Some of the station platforms also had roofs above the platform area. When a station float is tied up at a pier station a gangway is extended from the pier onto the barge to allow stevedores to unload and load cargo from the boxcars on the barge. The railcars are never removed from the barge, remaining 'at sea' during their entire period at the station.

---

[1] All of the locations in this material were linked to their parent's mainline facilities through the use of floating or marine equipment. What is perhaps one of the best discussions of railway marine equipment in the present author's opinion can be found in the book Taber, Thomas Townsend (deceased) and Taber, Thomas Townsend, III: **THE DELAWARE, LACKAWANNA & WESTERN IN THE TWENTIETH CENTURY – VOLUME II – Equipment and Marine**; published by Thomas Townsend Taber III; Muncy, Pennsylvania, 1981.

[2] In all probability the Central Railroad of New Jersey was a sub-tenant of the Baltimore and Ohio Railroad given the relationship between those two roads.

Wallabout Basin (continued)
The anchorages at the Wallabout Basin provided only for the tying up of the barges on the side which suggests that the cargo in the cars on the outer barge track were unloaded via the cars on the inner barge track. There was absolutely no trackage in the Wallabout basin area. In late 1941 the United States Navy seized the area of the Wallabout Union Terminal adding the land to the Brooklyn Navy Yard, the entire area was rebuilt under naval ownership.

Erie Railroad
On an unknown date the Erie Railroad established a freight terminal at the southwest corner of Lemon Street and the Clinton Street Extension (as shown on the map above). The date that the Erie Railroad occupied this facility is not known but it remained here, serviced by carfloats as there was no trackage at this facility. Like the Wallabout basin area, this facility was seized for the expansion of the Brooklyn Navy Yard in late 1941.

Baltimore and Ohio Railroad – New York, New Haven and Hartford Railroad
As a part of its program of acquiring the Staten Island Railway company in the latter years of the Nineteenth Century it appears that the Baltimore and Ohio Railroad purchased a tract of land at the foot of North 1st Street in Williamsburg adjacent to the Brooklyn Eastern District Terminal but separate from it. As both the Philadelphia and Reading Company and the Central Railroad of New Jersey had corporate relationships with the Baltimore and Ohio Railroad this facility has also had the names of those rail lines associated with it. There was trackage on two piers and along the waterfront between the two piers south of North 1st Street. The Baltimore and Ohio Railroad appears to have left this facility during the first decade of the Twentieth Century in favor of a terminal agreement with the Brooklyn Eastern District Terminal. It then appears that the New Haven Railroad took over occupancy of this location remaining there until the Bay Ridge terminal was opened on January 17, 1918.

There are no known pieces of motive power associated with this property; given the dates in question it is entirely possible that this yard was switched using horses.

New York Central System
We have already mentioned the pier utilized by the New York Central System in the Wallabout Basin area; but that is not the only part of the New York Central System on Long Island story. During the early days of World War I the freight rail transportation system of the country was perceived as breaking down by the Federal government. The result of this was the exigency of seizing all of the nations railroad lines as of December 28, 1917. A new Federal agency, the United States Railroad Administration ("USRA") was formed to take control of every aspect of railroading in the country from freight train operation to locomotive and freight car design. The head of this new bureaucracy was William Gibbs McAdoo, the builder of the Hudson and Manhattan Tubes and the son-in-law of President Woodrow Wilson. Under Federal direction the New York Central System was granted trackage rights over the Hell Gate Bridge and down the Long Island Rail Road's Bay Ridge Branch from Fresh Pond Junction to the Bay Ridge float docks[3].

---

[3] Other trackage rights changes under the United States Railroad Administration ("USRA") in the Long Island area included the re-routing of Baltimore and Ohio Railroad and the Lehigh Valley Railroad through passenger trains from the Jersey City terminal of the Central Railroad of New Jersey into Pennsylvania Station, New York City. As a result during this war time period equipment of both of these roads was serviced at Sunnyside Yard. The trains themselves would have been hauled by Pennsylvania Railroad electric locomotives from Manhattan Transfer. The Baltimore and Ohio Railroad returned to the Jersey City terminal at the end of the Federal control period on March 1, 1920; the Lehigh Valley Railroad remained in Pennsylvania Station, New York until it ended through passenger service on February 4, 1961.

THE SHORTLINE RAILROADS OF LONG ISLAND   PAGE 73

New York Central System (continued)

At Bay Ridge the New York Central had the right to interchange cars with all of the lines connecting whether by car float or by track. The Central never established an agency in Bay Ridge and when the railroads were returned to the control of the corporate sector on March 1, 1920 these trackage rights ceased to exist. There are no known photographs of New York Central trains on the Bay Ridge Branch and it is thought that these trackage rights were never used.

Pennsylvania Railroad

As part of the massive New York Pennsylvania Station construction project that virtually remade the landscape of Long Island, the Pennsylvania Railroad constructed the Sunnyside Yards in Long Island City. This facility which opened on November 27, 1910 became at one time the busiest rail passenger yard in the United States; but that facility had nothing to do with carload freight traffic so we will no longer focus on it. For our story we must move to an earlier time at a meeting of the Board of Directors of the Pennsylvania Railroad held on May 9, 1900[4]:

> "The Road Committee report that, at a Special meeting held this day, the President stated that the question of acquiring control of the Long Island Rail Road Company had been under consideration by himself and the Executive Officers of the Company. The business of Brooklyn is confined almost to the East River water front, where this company's terminal facilities are very limited in capacity. On examining into the best manner of extending them it was found to be very difficult to do so along the water, this led to an inspection of the lines of the Long Island Rail Road, when the conclusion was reached that they afforded the best, and in fact, the only means of increasing the facilities of this Company in Brooklyn. The tracks of the Long Island Rail Road now extend from Thirty-Fourth Street to Bay Ridge with the line extending into the centre of the City[5]. On them, freight depots, yards for carload deliveries, and coal and lumber yards can be conveniently located. These lines also afford opportunities for the erection of manufactories of all kinds requiring direct rail connections."

Despite the corporate intention to use the Long Island Rail Road as their terminal line on the east bank of the New York Harbor, the Pennsylvania Railroad had already established two yards of their own, one was in Manhattan and outside of the scope of this material. The other station was at the foot of North Fourth Street in the Williamsburg section of Brooklyn. This North 4th Street or Eastern District Station in Williamsburg apparently opened during 1895 and was located across the street from the Brooklyn Eastern District Terminal. This facility was connected to the mainline via a float bridge and there was a quite a bit of trackage here as it was a very active freight station.

---

[4] This passage is quoted from pages 474 to 475 of the following book:
Burgess, George H.; and Kennedy, Miles C. for the firm of Cloverdale and Colpitts: **CENTENNIAL HISTORY OF THE PENNSYLVANIA RAILROAD COMPANY 1846 – 1946**; The Pennsylvania Railroad Company; Philadelphia, Pennsylvania; 1949.
Missing from this passage is the fact that the Long Island Rail Road possessed a New York State charter, any railroad wishing a terminal within Manhattan at this time needed such a document.

[5] This wording is rather strange given it was written during 1920. It may refer to the then current leasing of the South Brooklyn Railroad which reached New York Harbor just south of 34th Street in Brooklyn. The 'City' in the same sentence only makes sense if it is interpreted as referring to Brooklyn.

Pennsylvania Railroad (continued)

The early steam motive power at this facility is not known; the ban on coal burning steam locomotives within the boundaries of New York City led the Pennsylvania Railroad to develop their first internal combustion railroad locomotives. Using a frame similar to that of an A5 0-4-0 steam locomotive a box cab structure resembling that of an electric locomotive was mounted; inside was a 400 horsepower prime mover and Westinghouse electric gear, Westinghouse traction motors powered each axle. Three locomotives were built in the Altoona Shops in the period 1928 to 1930; they formed a pool of equipment that along with Long Island Rail Road diesel electric locomotive 403 were used at North 4th Street and the Pennsylvania Railroad's freight yard in Manhattan.

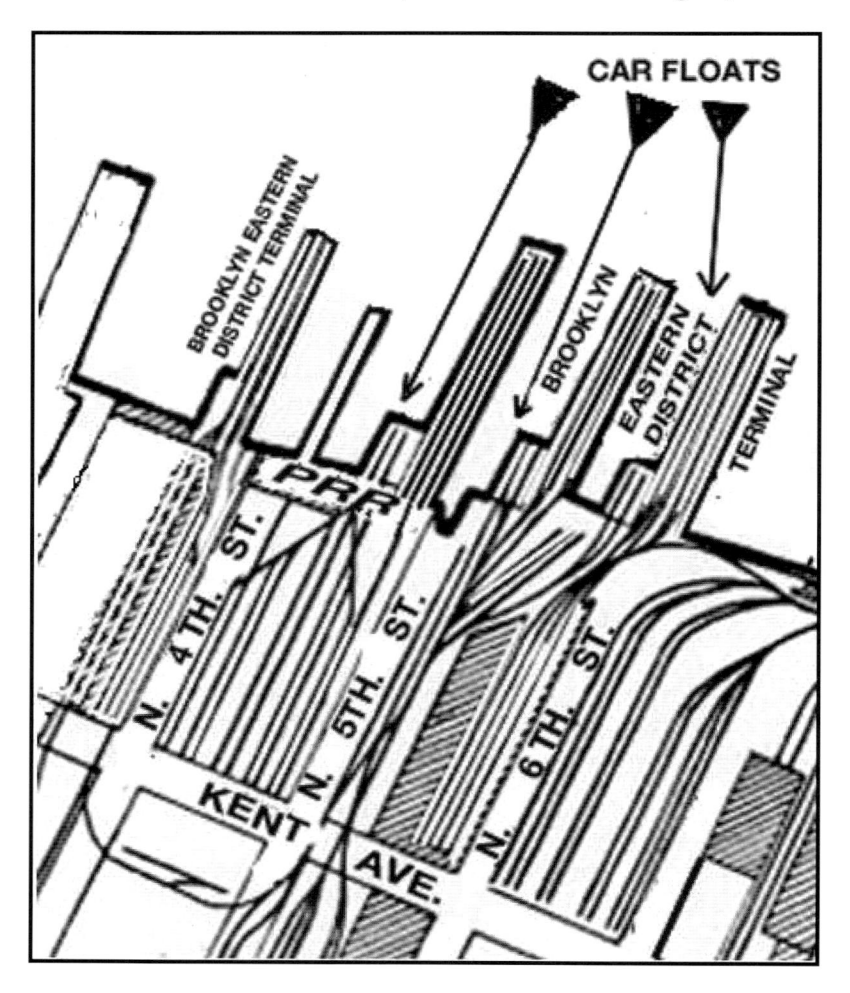

The Pennsylvania Railroad's North 4th Street freighthouse in Williamsburg is seen in this enlargement of George Wybenga's redrawing of the Army Corps of Engineers map of the Brooklyn Eastern District Terminal Kent Avenue area. Located adjacent to Kent Avenue and completely surrounded by the tracks of the Brooklyn Eastern District Terminal, there was no physical connection between the two railroads.

The North 4th Street Freight Station was sold during 1956 to the Brooklyn Eastern District Terminal company; under its new owner the facility continued to function until 1964-1965.

- * * * -

PENNSYLVANIA RAILROAD

The available photographs show only Pennsylvania Railroad 3906 and Long Island Railroad 403A as being physically at the North 4th Street Freight House but it can easily be assumed that other members of the Pennsylvania Railroad A6 class could have been rotated into this facility along with the Long Island Rail Road's other 'twin', the 403B.

While it was the 'Standard Railroad of the World'; the mighty Pennsylvania relied on nothing more that a typical consumer gasoline pump (to the left of the locomotive) to fuel the switching locomotive assigned to North 4th Street. This is the 3906 in an undated photograph by Frank Zahn from the Edward M. Koehler Jr. collection.

CLASS	NUMBER	BUILDER	SERIAL	DATE
A6	3905	PRR – Altoona Shops	4192	5/1928
A6	3906	PRR – Altoona Shops	4206	5/1928
A6	3907	PRR – Altoona Shops	4226	5/1930

These were three four wheel 400 horsepower boxcab gasoline electric locomotives with a Winton 148 prime mover[6] and a Westinghouse model 476 generator. The 3905 and 3906 were scrapped in 1953 and 1954 respectively. The 3907 was rebuilt during 1947 with a Hamilton 68SA diesel prime mover, it was re-rated to 450 horsepower and was re-classed A6b. The 3907 was retired during 1962.

- * * * -

---

[6] This was the prime mover used in the production models; the 3905 was originally built with another prime mover that failed to pass acceptance testing.

LONG ISLAND RAIL ROAD

The Long Island Rail Road's 403A serving as a relief engine at the North 4th Street freighthouse. The actual freighthouse structure can be seen at the left edge of the image. This is an undated photograph by Frank Zahn from the Edward M. Koehler Jr. collection.

CLASS	NUMBER	BUILDER	SERIAL	DATE
AA3	**first 403**	**Baldwin Locomotive Works**	**60185 to 60186**	**1/1928**

This was a two unit 'married pair' diesel electric locomotive consisting of two four wheel units with 330 horsepower prime mover powering Westinghouse electrical gear in each unit. Rebuilt in kind during December 1929 after which the two units were able to work separately, as such they were identified as 403A and 403B and nicknamed 'Mike' and 'Ike'. The 403A was taken out of service on May 17, 1944, the 403B on April 18, 1945. Both units were sold together to the Iron and Steel Products Company in Chicago; shipped to and stored at the Chicago Short Line's enginehouse. The Iron and Steel Products Company acted as a dealer and resold both units to the Standard Slag Company for use in a gravel pit in Crystal Springs, Ohio as their BLW60185 and BLW60186. The BLW60185 was used as a parts source. Both locomotives were scrapped in the last quarter of 1955.

- * * * -

A QUEENS' MYSTERY?
DEGNON TERMINAL RAILROAD
- * * -

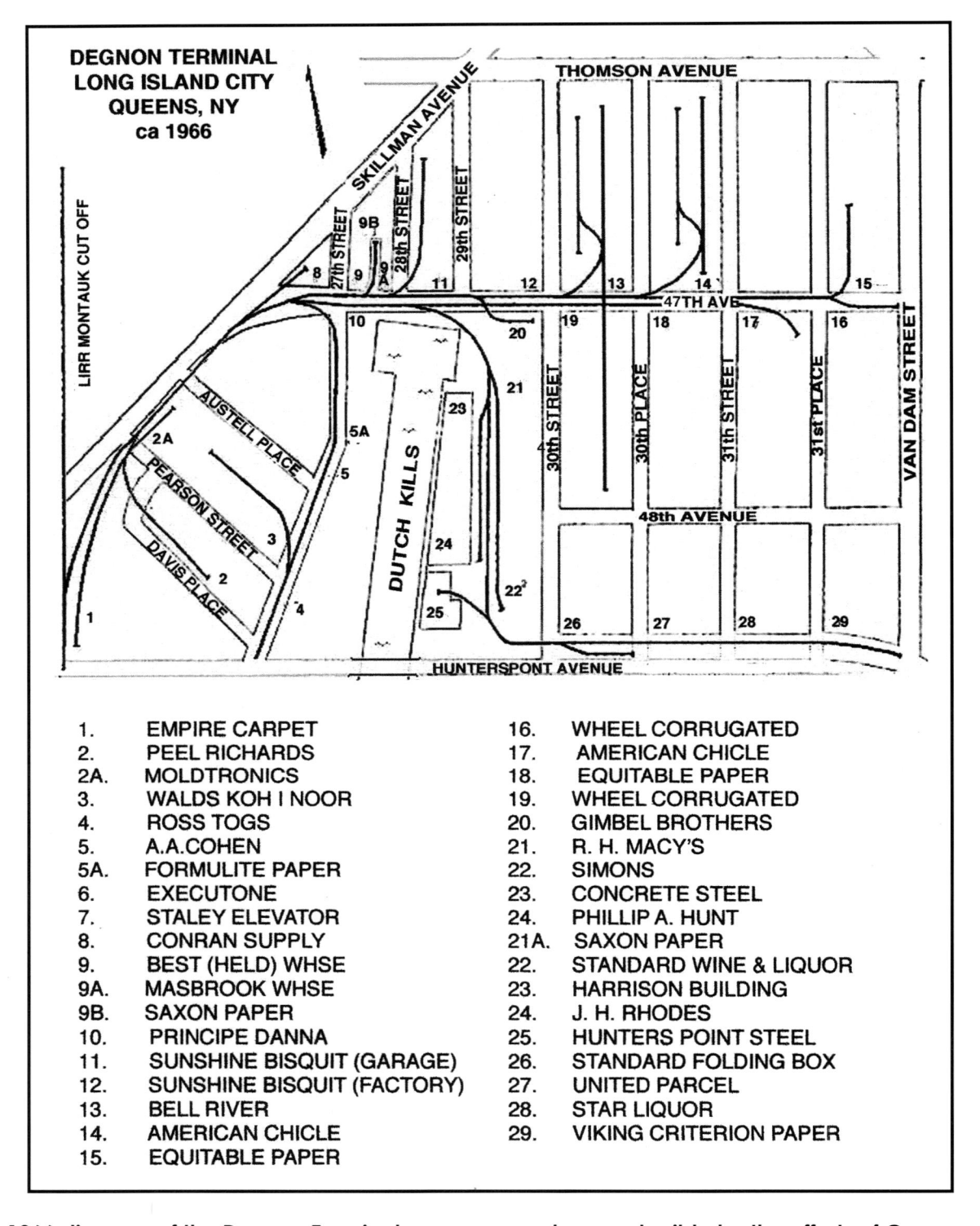

**DEGNON TERMINAL
LONG ISLAND CITY
QUEENS, NY
ca 1966**

1. EMPIRE CARPET
2. PEEL RICHARDS
2A. MOLDTRONICS
3. WALDS KOH I NOOR
4. ROSS TOGS
5. A.A. COHEN
5A. FORMULITE PAPER
6. EXECUTONE
7. STALEY ELEVATOR
8. CONRAN SUPPLY
9. BEST (HELD) WHSE
9A. MASBROOK WHSE
9B. SAXON PAPER
10. PRINCIPE DANNA
11. SUNSHINE BISQUIT (GARAGE)
12. SUNSHINE BISQUIT (FACTORY)
13. BELL RIVER
14. AMERICAN CHICLE
15. EQUITABLE PAPER
16. WHEEL CORRUGATED
17. AMERICAN CHICLE
18. EQUITABLE PAPER
19. WHEEL CORRUGATED
20. GIMBEL BROTHERS
21. R. H. MACY'S
22. SIMONS
23. CONCRETE STEEL
24. PHILLIP A. HUNT
21A. SAXON PAPER
22. STANDARD WINE & LIQUOR
23. HARRISON BUILDING
24. J. H. RHODES
25. HUNTERS POINT STEEL
26. STANDARD FOLDING BOX
27. UNITED PARCEL
28. STAR LIQUOR
29. VIKING CRITERION PAPER

This 1966 diagram of the Degnon Terminal area was made more legible by the efforts of George Wybenga for this publication. Note that the majority of the trackage in this area was either located in the street or along the curb line. The Long Island Railroad mainline and the Pennsylvania Railroad's vast Sunnyside Yards were located across Skillman Avenue from the Degnon Terminal area.

A QUEENS' MYSTERY?
DEGNON TERMINAL RAILROAD

Michael J. Degnon was a prominent contractor in the New York City area and was also influential in Queens County politics at the turn of the Twentieth Century. He was hired by the Pennsylvania Railroad to grade the land on which Sunnyside Yard was built. The work on Sunnyside Yard was performed by the Degnon Construction Company. The Degnon Construction Company had previously partnered with a similar firm owned by Colin McLean to build parts of bridges in the New York City area. Eventually the firm became known as the Degnon Contracting Company. A firm by the name of Degnon Realty and Terminal Improvement Company was formed during 1905 to build a series of industrial loft buildings located just to the south of the Sunnyside Yard complex. A total of seven hundred city lots were purchased along 47th Avenue from Van Dam Street to Skillman Avenue. On this plot of land a number of high rise factory loft buildings were erected which were served by a series of railroad sidings. The facility was not unlike Bush Terminal in Brooklyn. One feature of the Degnon Terminal area was the installation of elevators in some of the buildings that were capable of lifting freight cars to the floor of the consignee. In January 1908 the Degnon Contracting Company, who had utilized some 150 narrow gauge construction cars and ten locomotives (including two internal combustion locomotives!) in the building of the facility, turned it over to the Degnon Terminal Improvement and Realty Company. The day to day operations of the industrial complex did not require such a large roster of equipment nor were narrow gauge operations appropriate. The Degnon Terminal Railroad Company[1] was incorporated on November 18, 1913; the railroad received a franchise to occupy the streets in its service area on July 16, 1914 and the line was sanctioned by the State on July 27, 1914. The road had a projected opening date of January 17, 1917 and was expected to own 1.36 miles of track at that time. The acquisition of a 0-6-0 standard gauge steam tender locomotive solved the motive power issue for the little line.

The 'mainline' of this non common carrier operation branched off of the Long Island Rail Road's Montauk Cutoff adjacent to Skillman Avenue and then paralleled Skillman Avenue in an easterly direction turning into 47th Avenue which it followed to Van Dam Street where it ended. A 'branch' left the 47th Avenue 'mainline' and paralleled 30th Street towards Hunters Point Avenue where it turned west until it also reached Van Dam Street. The railroad track was not the only connection to commerce for the tenants of the Degnon Terminal, at the rear of the complex a barge canal[2] from Newtown Creek ended in a turning basin.

During a fan trip in the mid 1950's the Long Island Rail Road's Rail Diesel Cars made a photo stop in the Degnon Terminal area. This is a Paul Garde image from the Edward M. Koehler collection.

When the railroad operations of the Degnon Terminal were merged into the Long Island Railroad during 1928 no rolling stock was contributed to the larger road. The former Degnon enginehouse still stands near the intersection of Skillman Avenue and Forty-Seventh Street. The Long Island Rail Road operation into the Degnon Terminal area was usually performed on Monday through Friday by a train crew identified as Extra Crew 3.

---

[1] Technically as a non common carrier this line should be considered an 'Uncommon Carrier' but because of the merger with the Long Island Rail Road it is being treated as a terminal railway.
[2] The construction of this canal saw a drawbridge built to carry Borden Avenue over it; on this drawbridge were the tracks of the New York and Queens County Railway's Calvary Cemetery or Ridgewood line.

Extra Crew 3 reported to Yard A every weekday afternoon at 3:59 PM, their train already having been made up by the yard switching crew on the previous trick. The crew would then run from Yard A up onto the Montauk Cutoff and then down into the Degnon Terminal to perform switching moves as needed. Railroad operations in the facility tapered off and during the 1980's they ceased altogether. A caboose fan trip operated by the Long Island Sunrise Trail Chapter of the National Railway Historical Society on September 10, 1989 made an unsuccessful attempt to traverse some of the Degnon Terminal trackage. This became the last rail movement over the Degnon Terminal switch, it was taken out of service the following Monday and subsequently removed. Some Degnon Terminal trackage still remains in Forty-Seventh Street at present. One of the area tenants has had a former U.S. Department of Defense heavy duty flatcar positioned outside their store as an advertising gimmick.

(Left) Long Island Rail Road SW1001 number 103 switches a tank car full of chewing gum ingredients into the American Chicle Company factory on a rainy August 24, 1977. Image by Jeff Erlitz. The 103 would later have an important place in Degnon Terminal history.

(Right) A typical view of the Degnon Terminal area, while dating from a Sunday afternoon in February 1978, it is almost timeless when viewed as a black and white image. In the near distance the four stacks of the Pennsylvania Station New York's traction powerhouse stick up into the air; behind them is the Empire State Building. Image by Edward M. Koehler Jr.

(Left) Long Island Rail Road SW1001 number 103 struggles to lift a portion of the Long Island Sunrise Trail Chapter National Railway Historical Society fan trip out of Degnon Terminal onto the Montauk Cutoff on September 10, 1989. This was the last train into the Degnon Terminal; within days the switch would be taken out of service. Image by Edward M. Koehler Jr.

- * * * -

DEGNON TERMINAL RAILROAD

This roster is believed to be complete. It does not include the narrow gauge locomotives owned by the various Degnon contracting and construction concerns used in the area.

CLASS	NUMBER	BUILDER	SERIAL	DATE
	2	Schenectady Locomotive	5220	7/1899

This was a 0-6-0 slope back tender locomotive that was built for the Bellefonte Furnace Company, unknown number which was sold to the Degnon Terminal Railroad on an unknown date circa 1915 as their number 2. This locomotive was resold during 1924 to the Canadian Westinghouse Company as their number 4, passing to the Hamilton By-Products firm in November 1942. This locomotive may have been converted to a tank locomotive after leaving Degnon; no further information.

(Right) A little remarked upon feature of the Degnon Terminal property is the barge turning basin located at the 'rear' of the property. This is a view looking up the canal that connects this basin with Newtown Creek from the Hunterspoint Avenue drawbridge. Note the wharf on the left. This is a rather recent Edward M. Koehler Jr. image.

This image actually belongs to the 1958 Long Island Railroader article that is reprinted on the next page. Long Island Railroad Alco S1 number 406 switches one of the industries in the Degnon Terminal. This image is from 1958 and is from the Long Island Railroader. Unfortunately the fold line in this employee's newspaper goes right across the image.

- * * * -

LONG ISLAND RAILROADER

Volume 3, Number 9 of April 24, 1958[3]

THE LOCOMOTIVE THAT DOESN'T LEAVE HOME

Switching twenty-nine different industries on twenty four tracks concentrated in about a fifteen square block area is a challenging enough job. But when you have to move parked automobiles off the tracks, pull freight cars out in order to get past one industrial plant to reach another and do most of this in the dark – you've got a real problem. That's what goes on each night, when the diesel switcher hauling from twenty-four to forty cars into the Degnon Terminal from Yard A. One reason much of the terminal work is done at night is shown in the other pictures – the many streets are pretty well cleared of parked cars. Still the crew of J.G. Friedling, brakemen; T.G. Larson, conductor, Charles Sundheimer, Engineer; and J.E. Paladino, Fireman have to keep their eyes peeled for track obstructions.

(Above) In the gathering dusk Brakeman J.T. Cahill rides the engine catwalk keeping his eyes peeled for track obstructions. The line across the image is the fold from this employee's newspaper. This is a 1958 Long Island Railroad image.

(Above) The daily freight arrives in Degnon Terminal as a switcher shoves a cut of cars down the north lead track. This is a 1958 Long Island Rail Road image.

(Left) Engineer Charles Sundheimer and Fireman J.E. Palladino check over their locomotive before starting out on their nightly journey from Yard A. This is a Long Island Rail Road image from 1958.

- * * * -

---

[3] The original presentation of this story mixed the photo captions and the main text; as shown here the article has been edited to separate out the captions from the main text which has resulted in some minor re-wording to maintain readability and the original context.

THE LAST STREET RAILWAY IN KINGS COUNTY

THE SOUTH BROOKLYN RAILWAY

- * * -

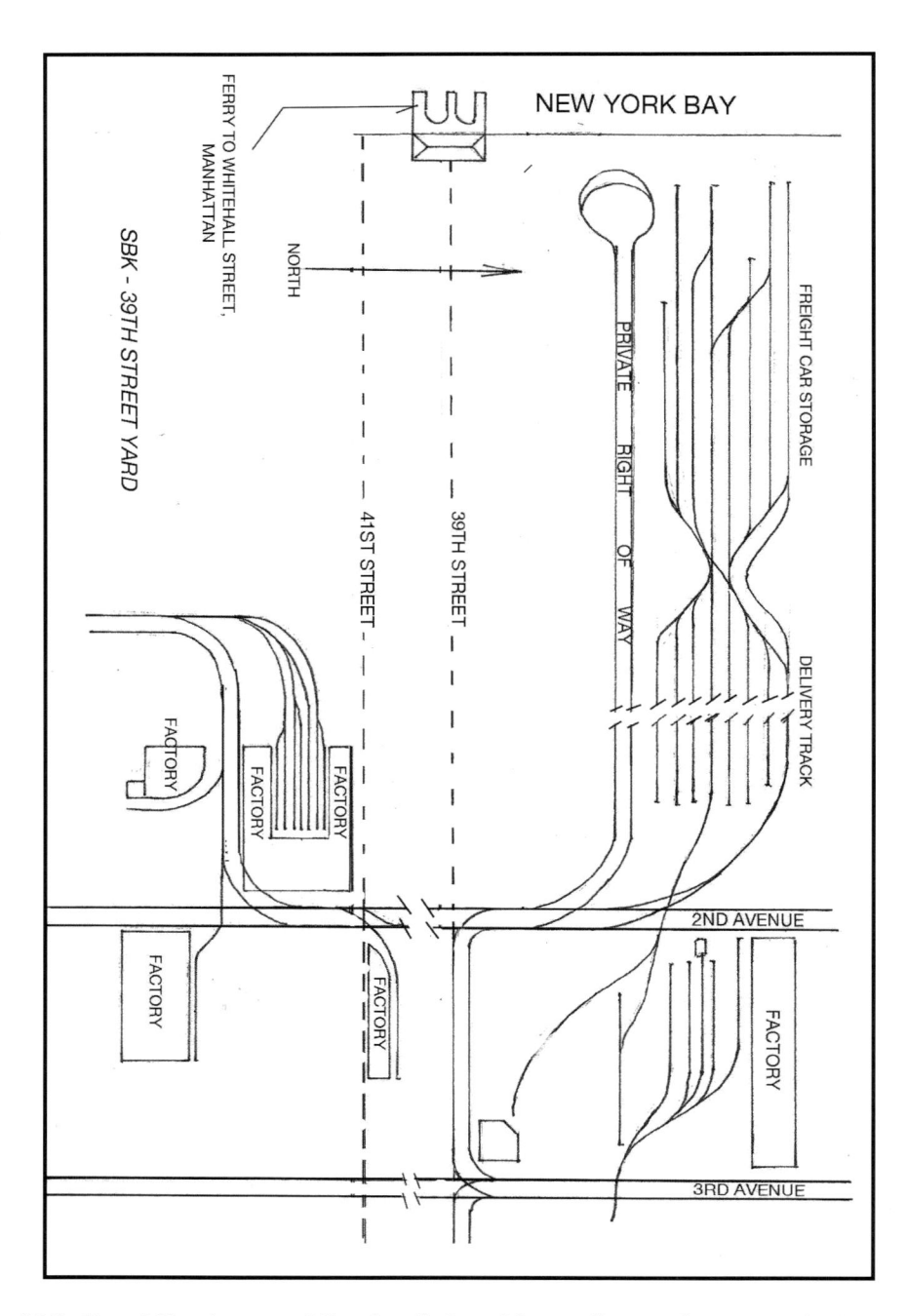

The 39th Street Yard area of the South Brooklyn Railway circa 1911 is shown in the upper right of this diagram from Robert Emery that has been redrawn by George Wybenga and turned 90° to fit the page. The loop track in the upper center was the terminal of the Church Avenue surface car line which continued to serve the site of the ferry to Manhattan long after the boats had ceased running. The trackage in the center left of the image belongs to the Bush Terminal Railway.

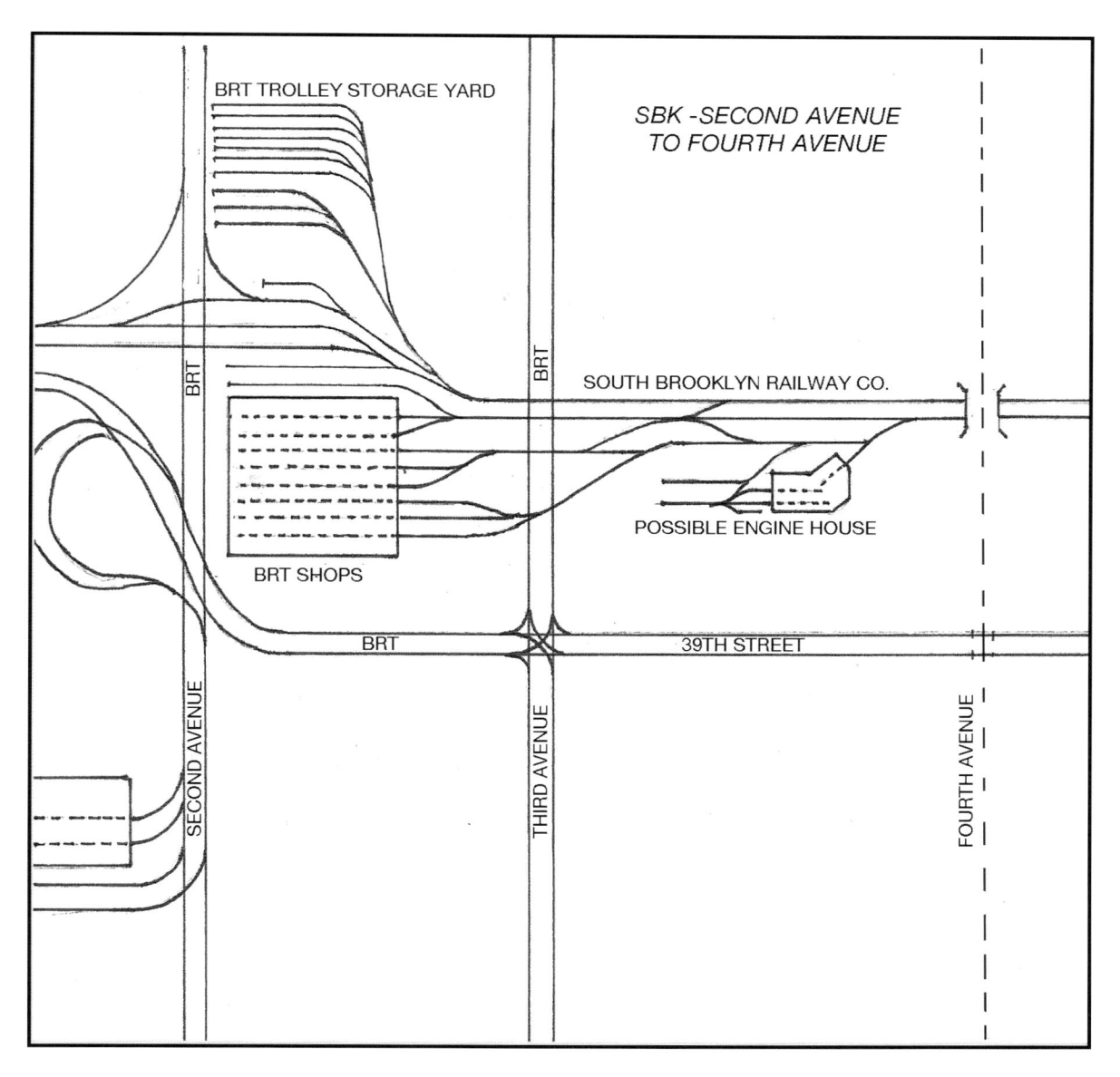

A track diagram from Robert 'Bob' Emery that has been redrawn by George Wybenga; this shows the South Brooklyn Railway trackage between Second and Fourth Avenues circa 1905. The 'Possible Engine House' shown center right is quite interesting, it does not show on later Brooklyn Rapid Transit era surface rail maps. Perhaps this facility dates from the period when the Long Island Rail Road was operating freight service over the South Brooklyn Railway and the Prospect Park and Coney Island Railroad. The massive Brooklyn Rapid Transit repair shops were located between Second and Third Avenues as shown in this map, officially they were owned by a subsidiary known as the Brooklyn Terminal Railway.

(Right) A 1940 vintage diagram of the South Brooklyn's Kensington Junction where the original South Brooklyn Railway was tied into the Prospect Park and Coney Island Railroad by the Brooklyn Rapid Transit. Note that this diagram and the one below on this page do not include the overhead elevated trackage of the Culver Line. The unused interlocking tower shown on the map stood as a lonely sentinel above the junction it once protected for many years, surprisingly it was little photographed. The original version of this track diagram was drawn by Robert 'Bob' Emery; it has been redrawn by George Wybenga.

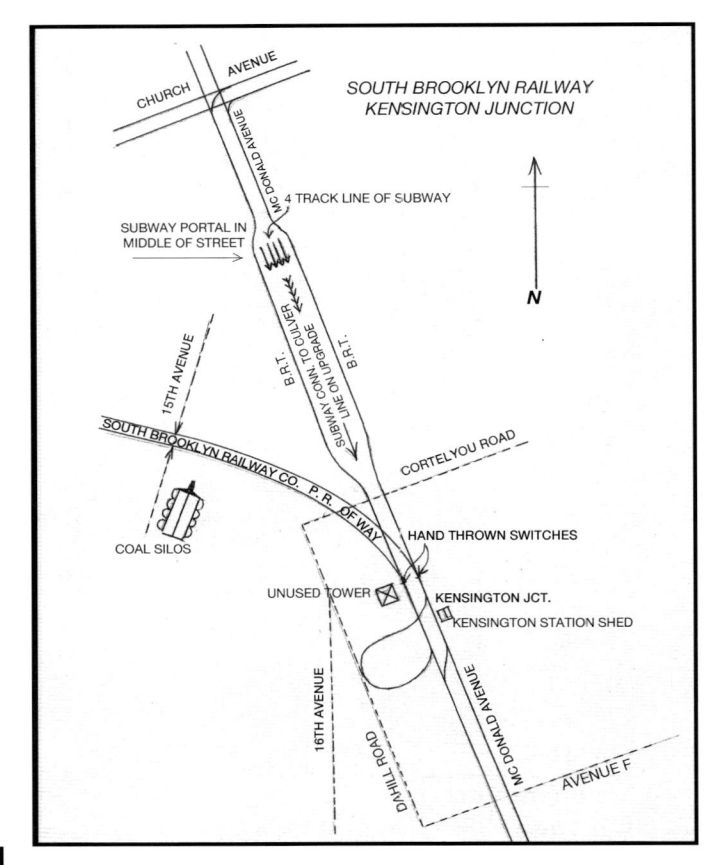

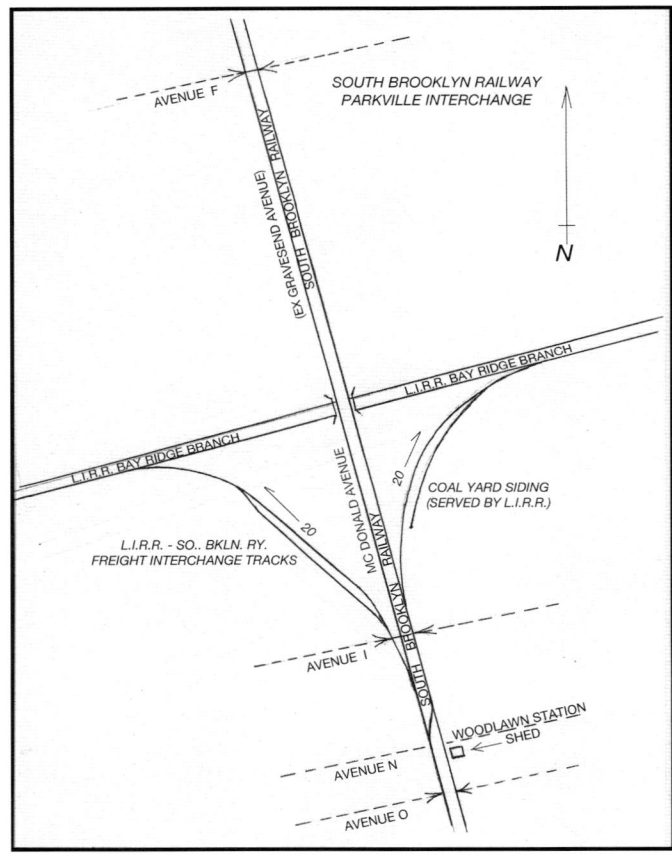

(Left) Parkville, the location of the interchange track between the South Brooklyn Railway and the Long Island Rail Road's Bay Ridge Branch. While the Gravesend Race Track which was located east of Shell Road (McDonald Avenue) north of Coney Island was hosting horse races, there was a Long Island Rail Road passenger service over the long gone and forgotten eastern leg of this wye. The original version of this track diagram was drawn by Robert 'Bob' Emery; it has been redrawn by George Wybenga.

THE LAST STREET RAILWAY IN KINGS COUNTY
THE SOUTH BROOKLYN RAILWAY

The Early Years

Today, the South Brooklyn Railway Company is a stepchild of the New York State sponsored Metropolitan Transportation Authority, but it was born on August 11, 1887 when the South Brooklyn and Flatbush Railroad Company changed its' name to the South Brooklyn Railroad and Terminal Company. Built in 1888 from the Thirty-Ninth Street Ferry Terminal to the intersection of Ninth Avenue and Thirty-Seventh Street, it was a pure speculation by the promoters among them W. Bayard Cutting and Joseph Richardson.

The line of rails intersected two major Brooklyn trunk lines, the Brooklyn, Bath, and Coney Island Railroad (today's West End line) at Fifth Avenue and the Prospect Park and Coney Island at Ninth Avenue (today's Culver line). The owners of the then titled South Brooklyn Railroad and Terminal Company had no desire to operate their own line as they had not even purchased equipment to do so! The real goal was to lease the property out to one of the aforementioned railroad properties and collect a nickel per passenger for the right to pass over the nine block line. Before one truly questions the sanity of the promoters of the Railroad and Terminal Company; remember that passengers on both the West End and the Culver line had to change to horsecars at either Fifth Avenue and Twenty-Seventh Street for the West End; or at Greenwood Depot for Culver line riders; to continue their trip into the then City of Brooklyn.

Sometimes one image catches your fancy; such a shot is this one of the 9980. This humble dump motor began its career with the Brooklyn Rapid Transit hauling construction and maintenance materials; perhaps going on to hauling loads for the Brooklyn Ash Removal Company to Barren Island. It finally ended up as the yard switcher at 39th Street. As the song in Broadway show Evita says "I shall never leave you"; so it is for the 9980, she is now preserved at the trolley museum in Branford, Connecticut. This image is from the Gene Collora collection via Robert Delmonico.

The ability to reach a ferry that could provide continuing service toward Manhattan and a wealth of additional passengers could be a financial boon to the line that achieved it, but not at a 5 cent a head penalty. Spurned by the two most obvious suitors, the South Brooklyn Railroad and Terminal Company sought marriage with the Long Island Rail Road by announcing its intention to build eastward to the Queens County border and on into Suffolk County. The management in Jamaica hardly blinked at this implied threat to their then sovereign Long Island. Indeed, this was the second of three times that a "southern route trunk line" would be proposed to be built east from the Brooklyn shore of New York harbor, and it always failed, even when the Long Island itself had tried it in the middle of the 1890's with the New York Bay Extension Railroad.

The West End line, meanwhile, tired of terminating in the middle of the street, helped in the building of the Fifth Avenue Elevated Railway that gradually was constructed to the intersection of Fifth Avenue and Thirty-Sixth Street, opening on May 30, 1890. Before this date, the Culver line chartered

The Early Years (continued)
the Prospect Park and South Brooklyn Railroad and built a branch from McDonald Avenue to Fifth Avenue and Thirty-Sixth Street which was shown in timetables as the "Fifth Avenue and Thirty-Sixth Street Division". The crowning touch where the three lines all came together was a large commodious structure called the Brooklyn Union Depot which opened on May 30, 1890 for West End trains and on June 7, 1890 for Culver trains. The South Brooklyn Railroad and Terminal Company was now actually paralleled between Fifth and Ninth Avenues by the Culver line; and effectively between the Ferry and the Brooklyn Union Depot by the Fifth Avenue Elevated which had the added advantage of serving various Brooklyn neighborhoods along the way to Manhattan.

Of all the lines discussed in this book, only the South Brooklyn Railway had an entry in the 1917 edition of the Official Equipment Register. But this information is only slightly helpful, note that despite it being a listing for the South Brooklyn Railway (reporting marks: 'SBK'), all of the equipment was physically lettered 'Brooklyn Rapid Transit'. The thin paper of this guide has allowed the Reading Company's information to bleed through in this image.

By all rights, the South Brooklyn Railroad and Terminal Company, now having lain unused for two years should have been ripped up as serving no real purpose and having no foreseeable future purpose; but it was now time for railroad politics to intervene. In Brooklyn, two spheres of influence were created, the Long Island Rail Road under Austin Corbin; and the Atlantic Avenue Railroad, later the Nassau Electric Railroad. The Culver line gradually came under the wings of the Long Island Rail Road, who would make it a subsidiary effective from January 24, 1893. The West End line and the Fifth Avenue Elevated gradually entered the other camp. The union in Brooklyn Union Depot was becoming an unhappy one and the Long Island began to crowd out the now 'enemy' West End line. This resulted in a lease of the South Brooklyn Railroad and Terminal Company effective from February 27, 1892 by the Brooklyn, Bath, and Coney Island Railroad. The West End line diverted every other train to the ferry terminal, bypassing the Union Depot to the southeast. After laying fallow and unwanted for four years, the little nine block long property, or at least the portion west of Fifth Avenue, finally became active. Austin Corbin and the Long Island Rail Road achieved total 'victory' in 1895 when on June 29th; all West End line trains were rerouted to the ferry.

The Brooklyn Rapid Transit

The South Brooklyn's 9421 was built to handle less than carload freight and express throughout the Brooklyn Rapid Transit surface system. Those days were past when this image of the box motor at the Canarsie carhouse was captured. This image from Paul F. Garde in the collection of Edward M. Koehler Jr.

As we alluded to before, the West End line had become part of the Nassau Electric Railroad combine which in later days was better known as the Brooklyn Rapid Transit Company ("BRT"), which even lives today as the inspiration of a National League baseball team name. The BRT as it was usually referred to, quickly converted the West End line and the South Brooklyn Railroad and Terminal Company to trolley car operation and tied it into the rest of the street railways in Brooklyn. This saw the South Brooklyn line between Fifth Avenue and the ferry reduced to a unwanted backwater operation. Elsewhere in Brooklyn, the Long Island Rail Road, with two lines to Coney Island, the Culver and the Manhattan Beach; was beginning to feel the pinch of the trolley competition and the nickel fare of the BRT. Rather than cut services, the Long Island sought to cut the cost of operating the service. For every passenger handled through Bay Ridge, the Long Island was paying the Staten Island Rapid Transit Company; the owners of the ferry franchise ten cents per rider. This dime penalty did not apply at the Thirty-Ninth Street Ferry so at the end of the 1897 season, passenger service was permanently withdrawn from the Bay Ridge terminal. Regular service would never run there again save for four trains a day during the summer of 1904 and the German 'boat trains' between the two World Wars.

The Long Island leased the South Brooklyn Railroad and Terminal Company from the Nassau Electric Railroad; grafted it onto the subsidiary Prospect Park and Coney Island Rail Road and began running seasonal passenger trains on June 30, 1898. This was also the date that a five year lease of the South Brooklyn to the Long Island became effective. While the lease was a benefit to the Long Island, the Brooklyn Rapid Transit also profited from the transaction. The payment that Jamaica was required to make was insufficient for the South Brooklyn Railroad and Terminal Company to pay its fixed charges so the little line slid into receivership. The property was sold at auction in December, 1899 to the Brooklyn Rapid Transit as the South Brooklyn Railway Company; pity the few minority shareholders left at that time. Meantime, the Long Island was not making any successful inroads on controlling the rising costs of the summer excursion roads so one of the two properties was deemed surplus. In the later part of 1898 the Long Island Rail Road began discussions with the Brooklyn Rapid Transit about their acquiring the Prospect Park and Coney Island Railroad. The BRT opined that it would be interested in the line if it were electrified so the wires began to go up in April of 1899. On June 17, 1899 the Brooklyn Rapid Transit became the leaser of the Prospect Park and Coney Island Railroad for 999 years, linking it with the Vanderbilt Avenue streetcar line. The Long Island Rail Road retained trackage rights over the Prospect Park and Coney Island Railroad and continued as the lessor of the South Brooklyn Railroad and Terminal Company under the five year lease dating back to June 30, 1898.

The Brooklyn Rapid Transit (continued)
Let us take a look at the South Brooklyn Railroad and Terminal Company at this time. It extended from the Thirty-Ninth Street Ferry Terminal up the hill in a cut; across Fifth Avenue and into the yards behind the Brooklyn Union Depot. Passenger service over the line was operated by steam trains of the Long Island Rail Road that came out of Manhattan Beach. These trains had traveled west (railroad direction) via the Manhattan Beach Branch; turned east (railroad direction) at Manhattan Beach Junction onto the Bay Ridge Branch and then at Parkville took a west to north (actual direction) curve onto the Prospect Park and Coney Island (approximately the location of the intersection of Avenue I and McDonald Avenue today). The South Brooklyn then continued west (railroad direction) on McDonald Avenue in the company of Brooklyn Rapid Transit trolleys; to Kensington Junction (today McDonald Avenue and Cortelyou Road) where the Long Island Rail Road steam trains threaded their way onto the branch to the Brooklyn Union Depot. Rather than pulling into that Brooklyn Rapid Transit facility, they jogged south (actual direction) across the yards onto the South Brooklyn line and eased down the grade to the ferry terminal. A Long Island Rail Road freight switcher crew was called for twelve hours daily except Sunday year round to work any tonnage on both the Prospect Park and Coney Island Railroad and the South Brooklyn Railway and Terminal Company.

Looking west from above the tunnel mouth at Fourth Avenue, 38th Street is to the right. The single BU type car on the elevated structure is servicing as the Bay Ridge Shuttle car. Undated image from the collection of Robert Delmonico.

The Brooklyn Rapid Transit, while owning the now reorganized South Brooklyn Railway, was not in possession of it due to the lease by the Long Island Rail Road. With the termination of the lease on June 1, 1903; it appears that the Long Island Rail Road discontinued passenger service to the Thirty-Ninth Street Ferry. The following season, 1904, the Long Island tested the waters regarding a revived combined ferry rail service to Manhattan Beach when it reopened the Bay Ridge Terminal, but the days of Manhattan Beach and Coney Island as a steam railroad operated resort had faded into the initials BRT. The Long Island would continue Manhattan Beach passenger service via East New York and Long Island City until 1924. The bright spot in that part of Brooklyn for the Long Island Rail Road was that daily twelve hour freight switcher! Business was booming on McDonald Avenue and in the vicinity of the Thirty-Ninth Street Ferry Terminal. The surface trolley passenger oriented Brooklyn Rapid Transit was uninterested in this service so the Long Island Rail Road continued to operate the freight switcher for two more years. In 1904 the Brooklyn Heights Railroad shops, a part of the Brooklyn Rapid Transit, turned out two steeple cab electric locomotives, and a third in the following year. While the author has no hard facts that these motors were for use on the South Brooklyn Railway and the Prospect Park and Coney Island Railroad for freight service, the discontinuance of the Long Island Rail Road service and the existence of the freight consignees on the properties past March 30, 1905 is fairly substantial evidence that the service did continue uninterrupted.

At this point, it would behoove us to look at the Brooklyn Rapid Transit Company for a moment. The BRT was a conglomeration of over eighty companies most of whose rolling stock was in the hands of a single holding company. The BRT owned no equipment or lines; it merely operated the system, and purchased the cars for the various underlying organizations. The cars which were specifically owned by one company were used system wide so it was entirely possible to see a Nassau Electric

THE SHORTLINE RAILROADS OF LONG ISLAND

The Brooklyn Rapid Transit (continued)

The previous image was taken from the bridge in the distance looking towards this photographer. The trackage was being rehabilitated in the 38th Street yard area in this image from April 7, 2012 by Edward M. Koehler Jr. A West End line subway train is just visible in the distance.

Railway car operated on the line to North Beach in Queens County. Thus the fact that these three steeple cabs were owned by their builder, the Brooklyn Heights Railroad, doesn't mean they stayed there. Indeed, the freight sidings of the Brooklyn Rapid Transit system extended from oil terminals in Mill Basin to pier side facilities on Varick Avenue. It was under the charter of the South Brooklyn Railway that the Brooklyn Rapid Transit began the aggressive expansion of freight service onto as many of the operated lines that justified it.

As the BRT began to convert the former steam lines it had acquired and consolidated terminals at various locations, more properties began to be transferred to the ownership of the South Brooklyn Railway. In March, 1907; the Sea Beach terminal grounds at Sixty-Fifth Street in Bay Ridge were transferred over to the South Brooklyn for use as a harbor side terminal. Two years later the south end of the Sea Beach line, the Sea Beach Palace, was also converted to a team yard. With track expansion there was a need for more equipment. The Brooklyn Heights out shopped another locomotive in 1907, this time a box cab (number 4) and from the start, her reporting marks were SBK for the South Brooklyn Railway. In 1910, the first 'store-bought' locomotive came to the South Brooklyn in the form of an American Locomotive Company car body with General Electric equipment, this steeple cab was numbered 5. It is believed by the author that the arrival of locomotive number 5 allowed the gradual transfer of the three original wood steeple cabs to duties elsewhere on the Brooklyn Rapid Transit system.

Two more steeple cab locomotives were acquired in February and March of 1914, but the first 6 and 7 lasted in Brooklyn but a short time as they were sold in December and October of 1917 to companies in Pennsylvania and Iowa, respectively. As we said before about Brooklyn Rapid Transit practices, these two locomotives were not actually owned by the South Brooklyn but by the Transit Development Corporation which was the BRT Company that owned some of the various shop facilities of the system.

While the Thirty-Ninth Street Ferry Terminal lost steam rail passenger service in 1903 with the withdrawal of the Long Island Rail Road; the Brooklyn Rapid Transit did continue to serve this location via a track constructed just to the south of the South Brooklyn line. This double track served as a route for the Church Avenue line; the West End line (prior to 1922); the Eighth Avenue line (after 1915); and as a rush hour only cut back of the Third Avenue line (until 1940). It was undoubtedly these vast trolley operations that justified the South Brooklyn Railway's acquisition of twenty Stephenson built double truck ten window semi-convertible trolley cars in 1907 numbered 2580 to 2599; an impressive roster for a company that offered no actual passenger service at that time! In reality, they were the last twenty cars of an overall order for one hundred cars, the balance going to the Brooklyn City Railroad as 2500-2579.

One of the most unremarked upon rail facilities in Brooklyn was the old Brooklyn Union Depot which continued to stand on Fifth Avenue into the mid 1980's; long shorn of its duties as a passenger terminal. This image is by Benjamin W. Schaeffer and was taken on April 22, 1983.

The Line down McDonald Avenue

There is a famous New York Central System publicity photograph entitled 'As Centuries Pass in the Night'. While not quite as dramatic, two South Brooklyn Railway train movements pass in the area of the 36th Street yard in this April 10, 1943 image from the Gene Collora collection.

To understand the next phase of the history of the South Brooklyn Railway one has to look away from the nine block line extending eastward from the Thirty-Ninth Street Ferry and into the background of the Culver line; better known as the Prospect Park and Coney Island Rail Road.

On May 18, 1870 the Park Avenue Railroad put a horse car line into service on Vanderbilt Avenue running from Park Avenue to Flatbush Avenue. The financial condition of the property was not good due to a dependence on a connecting line to reach the East River, and it soon was purchased by Andrew Culver who extended it. First order of business was an outlet to the East River which opened on May 1, 1871 via Navy Street, Concord Street, Gold Street, Front Street, Fulton Street, and Water Street. To be sure a long tortuous line, but, at least a line! Seven days later, the Park Avenue Rail Road was extended southward along what became Prospect Park West to Twentieth Street. With the northern part of what was to become the Culver line now in place, Andrew Culver set his sights on the beach at Coney Island.

On August 16, 1872 the Greenwood and Coney Island Railroad was incorporated to build a steam railroad from the south end of the Park Avenue Rail Road to Coney Island. In cooperation with the Town of Gravesend, Culver began construction along what is today McDonald Avenue (then Gravesend Avenue) from the intersection of Prospect Park West and Twentieth Street to Coney Island. With the roadway completed, track laying swiftly ensued down the center of the roadway. With the construction in hand, Culver began to simplify the corporate structure, merging the Park Avenue Rail Road and the Greenwood and Coney Island Railroad into the new Prospect Park and Coney Island Railroad on October 9, 1874. For test purposes the first train ran from Greenwood Depot to Gravesend Neck Road and back on June 19, 1875. The line opened for its' full length on June 27, 1875, the first line to serve the lucrative summer beach traffic. The company attracted the attention of the Atlantic Avenue Railroad which constructed a spur down Fifteenth Street from the Fifth Avenue line in an attempt to garner some of the connecting passenger traffic for its horsecars.

On July 4, 1878 the Brooklyn, Flatbush, and Coney Island Railroad opened a double track railroad from Empire Boulevard (then named Malbone Street) and Flatbush Avenue to Coney Island. Andrew Culver now had competition on the price and time sensitive seasonal traffic. The Prospect Park and Coney Island responded by rebuilding their line to double track and cutting fares below that of the new company, completing both goals in April of 1878; striking the next blow in the battle. The Culver property did have one ace in the battle though, the line served several small villages on the way to Coney Island, and the year round cash flow was nice to have.

THE SHORTLINE RAILROADS OF LONG ISLAND

PAGE 93

<u>The Line down McDonald Avenue</u> (continued)
The Culver line was extended from Coney Island to Norton's Point on June 9, 1879; this portion of the road was built under the corporate banner of the New York and Coney Island Railroad. This summer only operated subsidiary was leased to the parent Prospect Park and Coney Island on November 17, 1879. The line as it was then constituted consisted of a horse drawn street railway between Fulton Ferry and Greenwood Depot; a double track steam railroad down the center of McDonald Avenue to Coney Island, and a single track summer only shuttle operation to the steamboat pier down the back alley's of Coney Island and on out to the lonely steamboat pier at Norton's Point. On January 1, 1886 the horse car line north of Greenwood Depot was leased to the Atlantic Avenue Railroad, it was purchased by the lessor on May 27, 1887. While it appeared that Culver was cutting off his main source of passenger traffic, the Atlantic Avenue Railroad had been feeding traffic to him since 1875.

The South Brooklyn's second number 6 poses at a rather bucolic location believed to be opposite Greenwood Cemetery in the 36th Street yard in this June 21, 1942 image from the Gene Collora collection.

As related in the first part of our story, a new outlet for the traffic from Fulton Ferry, and indeed, all of downtown Brooklyn, was achieved with the opening of the Brooklyn Union Depot on May 30, 1890. The Prospect Park and Coney Island was purchased on behalf of the Long Island Rail Road on January 23, 1890; it became an operating subsidiary rather than being merged into the Sunrise Trail's corporate structure. When the Long Island Rail Road leased the South Brooklyn Railroad and Terminal Company from the Nassau Electric Railroad effective from June 30, 1898; it grafted the South Brooklyn's trackage between the Brooklyn Union Depot and the Thirty-Ninth Street Ferry onto the Prospect Park and Coney Island's branch from Kensington Junction to the Union Depot. The competition of the trolley lines nickel fare to Coney Island resulted in the Long Island throwing in the towel. On June 17, 1899, the Prospect Park and Coney Island was leased to the Brooklyn Rapid Transit for 999 years after the property had been electrified by the Long Island Rail Road using overhead trolley wire. The Brooklyn Rapid Transit continued to operate the line between Brooklyn Union Depot and Norton's Point using elevated cars of the well known BU type into the Twentieth Century.

Benjamin W. Schaeffer caught one of the two R47 diesels, either the N1 or the N2, heading westbound with two gondolas on the double track section that paralleled 37th Street on October 11, 1977. The steelwork above the train is the portion of the Culver line that was given over to the 'Culver Shuttle' in later years.

Transformation
The South Brooklyn apparently escaped the notice of the Federal Government and the United States Railroad Administration during the First World War as we can find no reference to the line's takeover. The City of New York did notice the rumbling wooden elevated cars however, and sat down with the Brooklyn Rapid Transit to convince it to modernize the operation. The modernization of the line took the form of an elevated structure; opened

Transformation (continued)

March 16, 1919 between the Brooklyn Union Depot and Kings Highway. The old Union Depot was replaced by a track connection to the Fifth Avenue Elevated allowing for through service. The station building was converted to a support facility for the system as a whole. The Brooklyn Rapid Transit did not rip up the original Prospect Park and Coney Island trackage under the new steelwork, but turned it over to the South Brooklyn Railroad to operate as a freight line. In addition, the BRT started operating surface cars along the McDonald Avenue portion of the South Brooklyn Railroad. The elevated line continued to be expanded to Avenue X on May 10, 1919; and on to Stillwell Avenue on May 1, 1920.

The South Brooklyn Railroad now consisted of the original line which started in a yard at the Thirty-Ninth Street Ferry and climbed the hill up to Fifth Avenue and there threaded its' way through the elevated yard until reaching a double track line under the Culver Elevated structure. The Culver line was duplicated on the surface in a private right of way until Kensington Junction was reached where the South Brooklyn Railway turned south and joined the double track surface car line down the center of McDonald Avenue near Cortelyou Avenue (Kensington Junction). At Avenue I (Parkville), a spur track descended down to the Long Island Rail Road's Bay Ridge branch for interchange purposes. At the intersection of Shell Road the line divided, one spur continued down the old Culver line right of way to the freight yard at the site of the Sea Beach Palace. The other leg continued south under the new steel overhead terminating in a team yard on the west side of Shell Road. Several years later, the Brooklyn-Manhattan Transit Corporation would build their Coney Island Shops at this location. A third leg was in existence, nominally in the name of the South Brooklyn, this double track line continued under the elevated structure to the Stillwell Avenue Terminal. It was used by the McDonald Avenue streetcars to reach their terminus. It also provided a connection to the Norton's Point Shuttle line whose ownership was also vested in the South Brooklyn Railroad. And so the Prospect Park and Coney Island Railroad name disappeared into the Kings County monolith known as the BRT.

The South Brooklyn lost trackage during this period at well; the Federal Government condemned the property at Sixty-Fifth Street and New York Harbor to use for the expanding Military Ocean Terminal in Bay Ridge. With the Bay Ridge yard gone, the connecting spur down from Third Avenue was no longer needed and was ripped up.

On January 31, 1978 the last delivery to the South Brooklyn's Parkville interchange took place. While it is in the Conrail era, perfectly Penn Central painted 9540 is about to drop off cars onto the siding. Meanwhile coming down the ramp trackage from McDonald Avenue is Sperry Rail Car 402 on its way to its next destination. This image is by Benjamin W. Schaeffer.

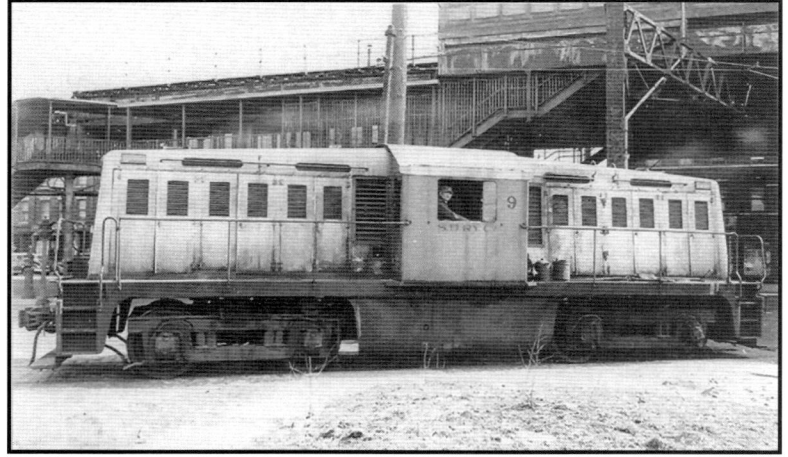

South Brooklyn Railway humpback Whitcomb diesel electric locomotive posed on the interchange track at Parkville in this undated image from the Joseph Testagrose collection. This is the opposite end of this spur track on which the Sperry car is standing as shown in the above image.

THE SHORTLINE RAILROADS OF LONG ISLAND

Transformation (continued)
The South Brooklyn had lost all passenger service with the cessation of Long Island Rail Road passenger service in 1904. With the new trackage, two trolley routes began to be operated over the South Brooklyn itself. The trackage in McDonald Avenue played host to Route 69 Gravesend-Vanderbilt Avenue which effectively reunited the old portions of the Prospect Park and Coney Island. This service terminated at the Brooklyn Rapid Transit's Stillwell Avenue facility in Coney Island. To the west of the Stillwell Avenue terminal along the alley known as Railroad Avenue under the elevated structure and then via a private right of way to Norton's Point beyond West Thirty-Seventh Street ran Route 74, Norton's Point.

From Kensington the South Brooklyn Railway proceeded south down the center of McDonald Avenue over a double track route that had been constructed by the Prospect Park and Coney Island Railroad which was better known as the Culver Line. The South Brooklyn Railway shared this trackage with the surface railways of Brooklyn. Here Brooklyn and Queens Transit 6001 is coming off of 16th Avenue while two unidentified PCC cars on the McDonald Avenue line are in the distance. This undated image is from the Robert Delmonico collection.

To provide sufficient passenger equipment for the two lines, the Nassau Electric Railway transferred six Birney cars to the roster of the South Brooklyn. While these cars could probably handle the winter loads on the Norton's Point line; what happened during the summer? Again, as with the twenty semi-convertibles of 1907, these cars were used throughout the Brooklyn Rapid Transit System.

Prior to the inauguration of Mayor Hylan and the resulting animosity between City Hall and the Brooklyn Rapid Transit, the BRT was successful in forcing the City of New York to allow it to participate in the construction of the subway system in the borough of Brooklyn. Indeed, the City had to rebuild the Fourth Avenue (Brooklyn) subway from Interborough Rapid Transit sized clearances to the bigger size of the BRT standard subway cars (better known as the 'BMT Standards'). On March 19, 1913; the so-called 'Dual Contracts' were signed; the immediate effect on the South Brooklyn was to be the elevation of the Culver line, a subject covered earlier. The December 31, 1918 receivership of the Brooklyn Rapid Transit had little effect on the South Brooklyn Railway. The electric locomotives continued to interchange with the Bush Terminal at Thirty-Ninth Street Ferry, the steeple cabs would strain up the hill to the Union depot yards, and then drill under the shadow of the Culver Elevated. During this period of financial instability, changes were mostly of a corporate nature. The Bankruptcy Court determined that the Nassau Electric was the true owner of the outstanding shares of stock of the South Brooklyn Railway. The Nassau Electric had contributed one piece of rolling stock during this period in the form of a General Electric steeple cab locomotive. The new

On December 23, 1964 Steven Rappaport caught a delivery train of class R32 subway cars moving on McDonald Avenue. Here is the 12, also numbered 20008 moving onto the lead to the Shell Road team yard.

Transformation (continued)

locomotive was the second to carry the number 6. It took the place of an earlier locomotive with the same number that had been sold to another line.

With the end of the summer season in 1922, the Norton's Point Shuttle operation was changed. The western most portion of the line beyond West Thirty-Seventh Street was reduced to summer only service. On October 23, 1923 the South Brooklyn became a part of the Brooklyn Manhattan Transit ("BMT") system. Again, there was little effect trackside for the subsidiary line. However, as work proceeded on the 'Dual Contracts' by a new entity, the New York Municipal Railway; the BMT convinced the City that there would be an increase of freight car loadings or work trains delivering supplies as a result of all this work. The proof of this was South Brooklyn Railway General Electric steeple cab locomotive second number 7 purchased from General Electric by the New York Municipal Railway. Except for the merger of the Nassau Electric Company into the Brooklyn and Queens Transit Corporation on July 1, 1929 which gave the South Brooklyn a new corporate parent, the late Twenties and Thirties were quiet and uneventful for the freight operations.

South Brooklyn 12 snakes the new subway cars into the Shell Road team yard in another of the December 23, 1964 sequence of images from Steven Rappaport.

The City of New York Steps In

On June 1, 1940, both the Brooklyn-Manhattan Transit and the Brooklyn and Queens Transit were merged into the City of New York through an exchange of stock. Payments by the City for this transaction were spread out over sixteen years, not ending until 1956. Municipal ownership brought about changes. Faced with repairing the bridge over Coney Island Creek, the City opted to build one block of track between the end of McDonald Avenue and the Norton's Point Shuttle. This new Shell Road trackage allowed the bridge to be dismantled.

In the final image of the December 23, 1964 delivery sequence from Steven Rappaport the train reverses from the Shell Road team yard onto the property of the New York City Transit Authority. Note that the diesel is carrying both the number 12 and 20008 on the hood end.

The City had plans to do away with the entire Brooklyn trolley network but World War II and a fleet of 100 relatively new Presidential Conference Committee ("PCC") cars worked against this rubber revolution. The first South Brooklyn Railway based target of the City was the partially seasonal Norton's Point Shuttle. This entire line was abandoned in favor of a new bus line on Mermaid Avenue effective from November 7, 1948. The shrinking of the trolley network elsewhere in Brooklyn created a pool of surplus equipment. Some equipment of note that ended up on the South Brooklyn Railway for additional service were two box motors utilized as sheds in the former Union Depot yards and a Treadwell dump motor of 1905 vintage. The dump motor was equipped with railroad type couplers and was used to switch the 39th Street Yard.

The City of New York Steps In (continued)

Most of the former surface trolley vehicles would join the collection of the Shore Line Trolley Museum in Branford, Connecticut between 1955 and 1965. While internal combustion buses were changing the face of the south end of the South Brooklyn, the new Transit Authority began a limited application of this technology to the north end of the property. Two Whitcomb humpback diesel locomotives, late of the United States Army, were purchased through the War Assets Administration. Numbered 8 and 9, these sixty-five ton units spent most of the careers on Transit Authority maintenance of way trains while the number 5, second number 6, and second number 7 usually switched McDonald Avenue. One of the Whitcomb locomotives was sold off in 1955, the year before all passenger service ceased over South Brooklyn Railway lines.

At the Coney Island Yard the South Brooklyn Railway's number 1 could be encountered. This locomotive, despite its ownership, was used by the Brooklyn Rapid Transit as a switch locomotive as the Coney Island Shops. The April 19, 1943 image is from the collection of Gene Collora.

Interestingly, it can be authoritatively argued that the line offered fully streamlined passenger service during the last years. The regularly assigned cars were the PCC cars of the former B&QT series 1000-1099 with their distinctive modern lines. On October 30, 1956 the 35 Church Avenue and the 50 McDonald Avenue lines were converted to rubber tire vehicles, but the wires remained overhead for freight service on McDonald Avenue. The 39th Street Terminal was dismantled and turned into a parking lot, the South Brooklyn locomotives being stored on the premises of Davidson's Pipe Yard adjacent to the old site and straddling the line. Three old four wheeled wooden box cars were purchased from the Singer Company and set out on the east side of the Third Avenue grade crossing to serve as a storage facility. The trolley wire was to remain intact until December 27, 1961, approximately a year after two used General Electric seventy ton diesel locomotives were placed into service by the Transit Authority. The passing of this era was marked with proper rail fan recognition. En-route to the Shore Line Trolley Museum in Branford, Connecticut was Sparvagar 71 late of Goteborg, Sweden. Unloaded from a flatcar on the Parkville interchange with the Long Island Rail Road, the rail fan trips on McDonald Avenue that day provided a nice Scandinavian send off to the overhead wire.

After the diesels took over, the second number 5, the second number 6, and the number 7 were equipped with third rail shoes and used on the Transit Authority for work trains, all three eventually being retained for historical purposes and they have been regularly exhibited in the Transit Exhibition which opened in 1977.

Getting back to the post 1960 period, the Transit Authority abandoned service on McDonald Avenue and Shell Road south of the team tracks located on the east side of the Coney Island Shops. The sixties had seen a flight of industrial concerns from McDonald Avenue as well as the

The City of New York Steps In (continued)
entire City of New York. The main problem was a simple lack of reasonably priced space for expansion, while the businesses remaining were of the nature that would have received less than carload shipments; that service no longer existed.

A scrapper, Sarnelli, leased the Shell Road Team Yard to process former New York City Transit Authority and Long Island Rail Road cars, but these movements were temporary at best. By 1972, there were few consignees left on the property, among them the parent New York City Transit Authority at Coney Island and the old Union Depot; a food processing plant on McDonald Avenue; and Davidson's Pipe Yard adjacent to the Bush Terminal interchange. The Parkville interchange with the Penn Central, while intact, existed mostly in theory only and the street trackage was in poor shape. Abandonment of the entire property would not have been a shocking development.

Instead the New York City Transit Authority replaced the two diesel locomotives with two new ones of their standard General Electric forty-seven ton design. Numbered N1 and N2, they sent the two older units (numbers 12 and 13) into storage and eventual resale. The New York City Department of Transportation undertook to rebuild and repave McDonald Avenue. This project included new double tracks for the line, but strangely not for the last one hundred yards into the Shell Road Yard - Coney Island Shop complex. This omission reduced the McDonald Avenue trackage from a mainline to a long straggling dead end spur with little economic purpose. The South Brooklyn Railway received trackage rights over the West End line from the old Brooklyn Union Depot to the Coney Island Shops to continue to serve their largest consignee and owner.

One other development of note was the creation of a herald for the South Brooklyn Railway. When the two new General Electric diesels were placed in service each had a silver circle with a two tone blue M for the Metropolitan Transportation Authority on the side of the cab. Underneath the M were the letters SBK for the South Brooklyn. Maybe not the most inspired design, but after eighty-six years of existence, a deserved acquisition.

With the formation of Conrail and their continued downgrading of the former Bay Ridge line, the Transit Authority effectively replaced the Parkville interchange with a new track connection between the Canarsie line and Conrail's Bedford Secondary Track south of East New York. The last delivery to Conrail at Parkville took place on January 31, 1978. The adjacent property owner quickly paved over the connecting track at Avenue I and McDonald Avenue for a parking lot rendering it out of service. The trackage between the Transit Authority's Coney Island Shops and the old Brooklyn Union Depot's 36th Street yard saw a clean up train removing all foreign line equipment on February 1, 1978. The one hundredth year of this road's existence has seen a form of renaissance on the line. True, the former Prospect Park and Coney Island trackage grafted onto the property had no current economic viability or future; but the original portion of the line between the Bush Terminal, now the New York Cross Harbor Railway and the old Brooklyn Union Depot saw daily operations. The New York City Transit Authority had begun a program of using outside shops to rebuild a large percentage of the cars on the system. As a result, a tremendous number of cars were passing over the line twice between 1987 and 1991. Another source of traffic was new subway cars being delivered to the Transit Authority at the Coney Island Shops.

During the 1988 closing of the Williamsburg Bridge, which isolated the Eastern Division of the Brooklyn-Manhattan Transit lines from the rest of the system, the South Brooklyn ran weekly shop trains from the Coney Island Shops to the Canarsie line via the West End line, the South Brooklyn, the Bush Terminal section of the New York Cross Harbor, and then the Bay Ridge line of the Long Island Rail Road to the Canarsie connection.

Beyond Transformation

What of the future? Well the current rebuilding program will see subway cars in a daily move in each direction over the line until 1991 and the Transit Authority undoubtedly could have more rebuilding programs starting up after that. There is always the chance that some sort of industry will locate on McDonald Avenue, but the "not in my neighborhood" syndrome works against that hope. Today's South Brooklyn, effectively a 'captured' common carrier working for its corporate parent, will probably continue on in some form of existence.

The preceding paragraph was originally written in the late 1980's or early 1990's and the optimism was unfortunately misplaced. The small segment of the South Brooklyn Railway west of Fourth Avenue saw very limited use, the outside rebuilders having trouble meeting New York City Transit Authority specifications on some of the work being performed. The interchange trackage with the former Bush Terminal Railway was removed from service and as the first decade of the Twenty-First Century ended the 39th Street yard was paved over to form an automobile storage yard. The trackage west of Third Avenue, while it continued to exist, became increasingly rusty. Perhaps a 2006 fan trip with South Brooklyn Railway number 5 at one end and South Brooklyn Railway number N1 sandwiching a former Brooklyn Manhattan Transit three unit D Type Triplex car was the last hurrah for the South Brooklyn; only history yet to be written shall tell . . .

An interesting view from the Gene Collora collection. This November 15, 1941 image was captured in the 39th Street yard near the interchange with the Bush Terminal Railway. In the view is electric locomotive number 5, to its rear is the 9980, a 1905 dump motor built by the Treadwell firm which was used to switch this yard; behind them both is box motor 9441 a 1905 product of the Laconia Car Company which was probably used more for storage at this date.

- * * * -

(Right) The Shell Road Yard area of the South Brooklyn Railway in a 1940 vintage track diagram from Robert 'Bob' Emery that has been redrawn by George Wybenga. The Brooklyn Manhattan Transit's (now the New York City Transit Authority's) vast Coney Island Shops (not shown) are located to the left of the trackage in this image. The eastern leg of the South Brooklyn Railway went to the site of the Sea Beach Palace; at this time it served as a freight station for the South Brooklyn Railway. The trackage on Shell Road continued into Coney Island before turning west and heading to Norton's Point.

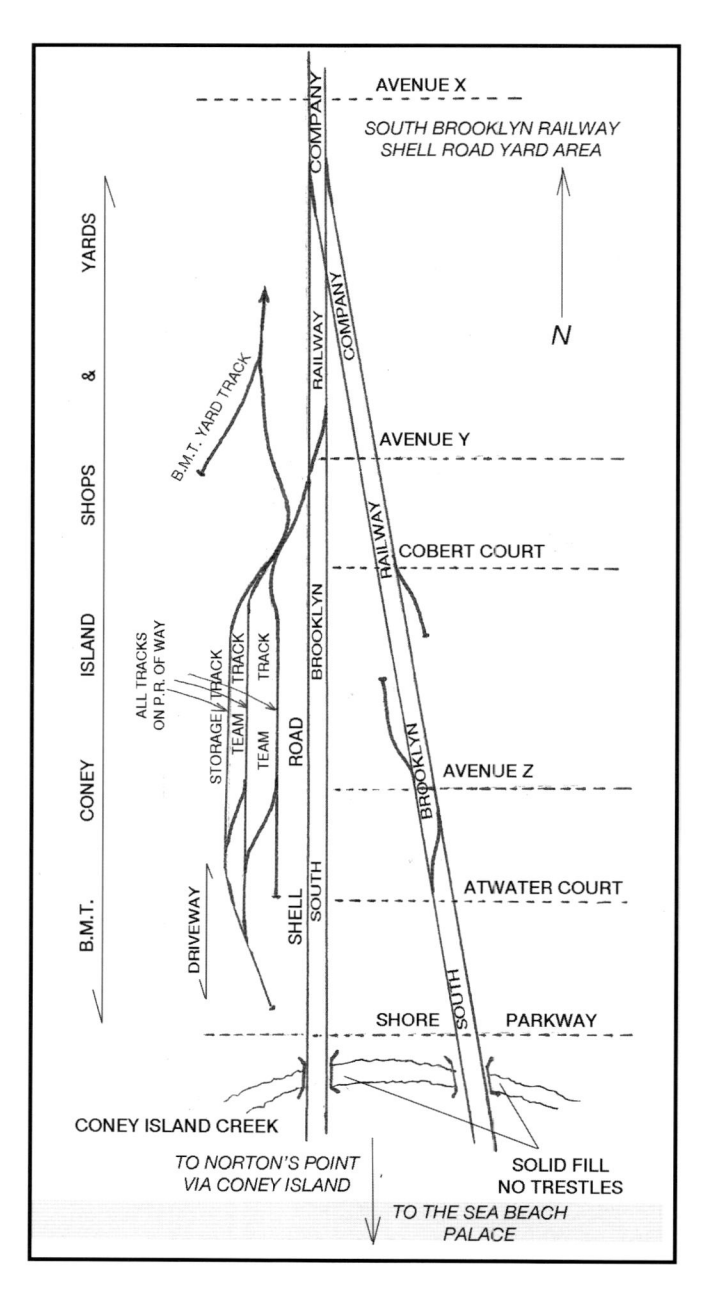

SOUTH BROOKLYN RAILWAY

CLASS	NUMBER	BUILDER	SERIAL	DATE
	1 to 2	Brooklyn Heights Railroad		__/1904
	3	Brooklyn Heights Railroad		__/1905

These were thirty-four ton steeple cab 600 volt direct current locomotives which were owned by the Brooklyn Heights Railroad; actual ownership of these three locomotives was probably never transferred to the South Brooklyn Railway. A photograph shows one of these locomotives working in the Brooklyn Rapid Transit's East New York car yard in 1915. The number 1 was retired in March 1955; the number 2 during 1947; and the number 3 in June 1954; respectively.

Although clearly lettered 'Coney Island Shops' in this undated image from the Gene Collora collection, the number 1 was supposedly built for service on the South Brooklyn Railway; it is seen here at the Coney Island Shops, the McDonald Avenue elevated structure is in the distant rear. The sister number 3 is known to have worked at the East New York complex of the BRT.

The boxcab number 4, like its three predecessors, was built in house by the Brooklyn Heights Railroad. The locomotive passed into the ownership of the City of New York later being renumbered 20001. It is now preserved at the trolley museum in Branford, Connecticut. This image is from the Gene Collora collection and was captured on June 5, 1943.

| | 4 | Brooklyn Heights Railroad | | __/1907 |

This was a fifty-seven ton box cab 600 volt direct current electric locomotive, placed in storage at the Coney Island Shops during 1955, renumbered to New York City Transit Authority 20001 in May 1962, supposedly back to 4 during 1966 but it was stored in Coney Island lettered 20001. This locomotive was transferred to the Branford Trolley Museum after 1980.

| | 5 | Alco – General Electric | 48559 | __/1910 |

This is a fifty-six ton steeple cab 600 volt direct current locomotive which also had General Electric builder's number 3266. This locomotive was transferred to the New York City Transit Authority in 1960 as their 5, renumbered to NYCTA 20002 in May 1962, and then back to NYCTA 5 during 1966. This locomotive is currently a part of the Transit Authority's museum collection.

| | **first 6** | **General Electric** | **4621** | **2/1914** |

This was a fifty-five ton steeple cab 600 volt direct current locomotive with a Wason car body. This locomotive was purchased by the Transit Development Company (a subsidiary of the Brooklyn Rapid Transit). This locomotive was sold in December 1917 to the West Side Street Railway (in Charleroi, Pennsylvania) as their (probable) 6; subsequently resold to the Niagara, Saint Catherine's, and Toronto as their 20 during 1937, eventually becoming Canadian National Electric Lines 20 as a result of a December 31, 1958 merger. Retired in November 1960 and scrapped in March 1961.

SOUTH BROOKLYN RAILWAY (continued)

CLASS	NUMBER	BUILDER	SERIAL	DATE
	second 6	General Electric	7280	4/1921

This is a fifty-two ton steeple cab 600 volt direct current locomotive that was purchased by the New York Rapid Transit Company, the joint Brooklyn Rapid Transit – City of New York enterprise that built the 'Dual Contracts' rapid transit lines operated by the BRT/BMT. This locomotive was transferred to the New York City Transit Authority during 1960 as their 2nd 6, renumbered NYCTA 20006 in March 1962, back to second 6 during 1966. Currently this locomotive is a member of the Transit Authority's museum collection.

This undated view of the number 5 comes from the collection of Gene Collora. The location of this image is believed to be in the area of the Coney Island Shops. This locomotive is in the Transit Authority's historical collection.

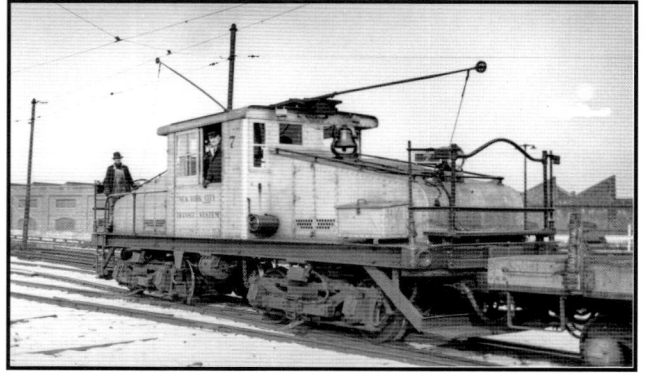

South Brooklyn Railway second number 7 was the highest numbered electric locomotive purchased for the line. This December 16, 1942 image is from the collection of Gene Collora; the location is not known.

| | first 7 | General Electric | 4622 | 3/1914 |

This was a fifty-five ton steeple cab 600 volt direct current locomotive with a Wason car body. This locomotive was purchased by the Transit Development Company (a subsidiary of the Brooklyn Rapid Transit). This locomotive was sold in October 1917 to Iowa's Inter Urban Railway as their 806; it became Des Moines and Central Iowa 1806 as a result of 1922 merger. This locomotive was caught in a car house fire during 1950 and scrapped due to the damage.

| | second 7 | General Electric | 9946 | 12/1925 |

This is a fifty-two ton steeple cab 600 volt direct current locomotive which was purchased by the New York Rapid Transit Company, the joint Brooklyn Rapid Transit – City of New York enterprise built the 'Dual Contracts' rapid transit lines operated by the BRT/BMT. This locomotive was transferred to the New York City Transit Authority during 1960 as their second 7, renumbered NYCTA 20004 in March 1962, back to second 7 during 1966. This locomotive is currently a part of the Transit Authority's museum collection.

THE SHORTLINE RAILROADS OF LONG ISLAND

SOUTH BROOKLYN RAILWAY (continued)

CLASS	NUMBER	BUILDER	SERIAL	DATE
	8	Whitcomb	60353	12/1943
	9	Whitcomb	60336	10/1943

These are two sixty-five ton 'humpback' diesel electric locomotives that were built as United States Army 7983 and 7966, sold by the War Assets Administration during 1947 to the South Brooklyn Railway as their 8 and 9. Locomotive 8 was transferred to the New York City Transit Authority as their 8 on an unknown date, renumbered to NYCTA 20005 in March 1962 and then back to 8 during 1966; transferred to the Staten Island Rapid Transit Operating Authority ("SIRTOA") as their 8 during 1971, retired during the last quarter of 1987 and stored. Locomotive 9 was sold September 1955 to the Newtown Iron and Steel (dealer in Jamaica, New York), who resold it in December 1955 to the Greenville Electric Manufacturing Works, Greenville, Ohio who rebuilt the unit before selling it to American Aggregates as their Brighton, Michigan number 9.

The former U.S. Army Transportation Corps 7983 became the South Brooklyn Railway's number 8, initially sporting a silver paint scheme with a maroon cab and frame. While not the sharpest of images, it is clear that the number 8 in this circa 1955 image from the collection of Philip M. Goldstein is moving out of the Bush Terminal interchange area with a freight train in tow. Note that the overhead wires are still in place.

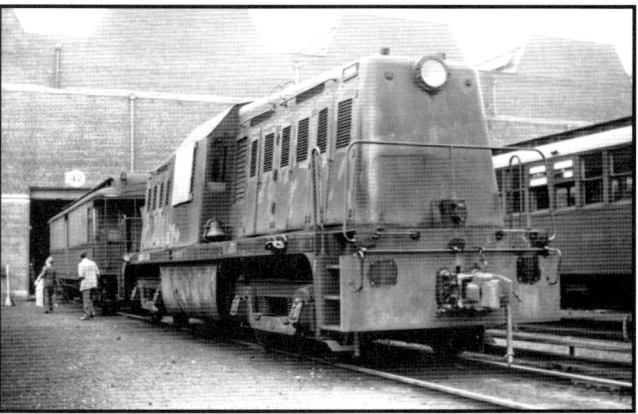

U.S. Army Transportation Corps 7966 soon after its delivery to the City of New York and before becoming South Brooklyn Railway 9. This sixty-five ton unit shows evidence of being prepared for operation in the European Theatre of operations, note the blotches where the buffers have been removed on the pilot. This image dates from November 1946(?) and is from the collection of Gene Collora.

	12	General Electric	30021	8/1948

This is an end cab seventy ton diesel electric locomotive that was built as Grafton and Upton Railroad 12, transferred in July 1954 to the related Claremont and Concord Railroad 12; during this period the locomotives cab was cut down for unknown clearance reasons. This locomotive was sold to the South Brooklyn as their 12 in November 1960. This locomotive was renumbered to South Brooklyn 20008 in March 1962, and back to 12 during 1966. Stored in December 1974 and subsequently resold to Naparano Iron and Steel who leased out the unit; its present status is believed to have been scrapped.

SOUTH BROOKLYN RAILWAY (continued)

CLASS	NUMBER	BUILDER	SERIAL	DATE

South Brooklyn Railway number 12 standing in the yards of the north end of the railway. This image was taken by the late Frank Zahn and is from the collection of Philip M. Goldstein. Notice the cut down cab on this locomotive as compared to the number 13 on the right.

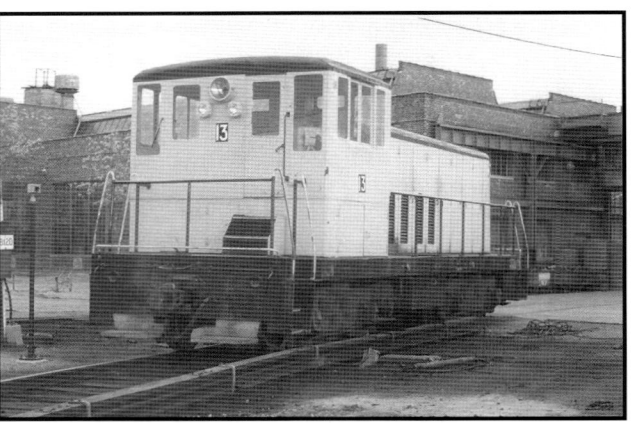

The number 13 standing in the Coney Island Shops of the parent New York City Transit Authority. This locomotive, like the sister 12, had been purchased used from the New England railways once operated by Samuel Pinsley. This image is by Joseph Torregrose.

| | 13 | General Electric | 28239 | 10/1946 |

This is an end cab seventy ton diesel electric locomotive that was built as Saratoga and Schuylerville 11, transferred during 1954 to the related Claremont and Concord Railroad 11; to the related Montpelier and Barre as their 23 during 1957 and in 1959 to the related Hoosac Tunnel and Wilmington as their 23. This locomotive was resold to the South Brooklyn in November 1960 becoming 13; became South Brooklyn 20009 in March 1962 and then back to 13 in during 1966. This locomotive was stored as of October 1974 and resold to Naparano Iron and Steel who sold the unit in December 1981 to the Thurso Valley Railway in Canada. Reportedly out of service after June 1986.

| | 20004 | General Electric | 9946 | 12/1925 |

See second number 7 for full information

| | 20005 | Whitcomb | 60353 | 12/1943 |

See second number 8 for full information

| | 20006 | General Electric | 7280 | 4/1921 |

See second number 6 for full information

| | 20008 | General Electric | 30021 | 8/1948 |

See number 12 for full information.

| | 20009 | General Electric | 28239 | 10/1946 |

See number 13 for full information.

| R47 | N1 | General Electric | 38946 | 10/1974 |
| R47 | N2 | General Electric | 38947 | 10/1974 |

These are end cab forty-seven ton diesel electric locomotives built to the standard New York City Transit Authority design for diesel electric locomotives, currently in service.

| | 2580 to 2599 | Stephenson | | __/1907 |

These are ten window double truck semi-convertible 600 volt direct current trolley cars used throughout the Brooklyn Rapid Transit system. The last survivors of this series of cars which totaled one hundred cars numbered from 2500 to 2599 were retired between 1945 and 1949.

THE SHORTLINE RAILROADS OF LONG ISLAND   PAGE 105

SOUTH BROOKLYN RAILWAY (continued)

CLASS	NUMBER	BUILDER	SERIAL	DATE
	7200 to 7205	Cincinnati	2395	3/1919

These are six 'Birney' design 600 volt direct current single truck cars that were built as Nassau Electric first 7100 to 7105, transferred to the South Brooklyn Railway as 7200 to 7205 upon delivery. Used throughout the Brooklyn Rapid Transit system. Car 7203 was sold to the Bush Terminal Railway during 1933 becoming their third 1; cars 7200 to 7202 and 7204 to 7205 were taken out of service by 1935.

On July 29, 1977 the N1 was found towing some newly delivered R46 subway cars through the grounds of Davidson's Pipe Yard by Benjamin W. Schaeffer.

During February 1978 Benjamin W. Schaeffer caught the N2 standing in the engine siding west of Third Avenue and located in the middle of Davidson's Pipe Yard.

| | 9121 | Baltimore Steel Car | | __/1904 |

This is a double truck 600 volt direct current motorized gondola car used to switch the 39th Street Yard; this car was sold to the Branford Trolley Museum in 1955.

A second view of the 9421, this one is near the end of its career on the South Brooklyn when it was serving as a storage shed near 39th Street. This image is from Paul Garde and is from the Edward M. Koehler Jr. collection.

The late Richie Harrison caught this view of the 9424 sitting in the 36th Street yard in May 1954. Behind it can be seen some of the Brooklyn and Queens Transit work equipment and cranes that survived into New York City Transit ownership.

SOUTH BROOKLYN RAILWAY (continued)

CLASS	NUMBER	BUILDER	SERIAL	DATE
	9408 to 9428	**Middletown Car**		__/1903

These are twenty-one double truck 600 volt direct current box motors that were used in less than carload freight service throughout the entire Brooklyn Rapid Transit system. Of this group of cars the 9421 and 9425 survived to be used as storage sheds in the former Brooklyn Union Depot yard area. The 9421 and 9425 were sold to the Branford Trolley Museum.

| | **9429 to 9443** | **Laconia Car** | | __/1905 |

These are fifteen double truck 600 volt direct current box motors that were used in less than carload freight service throughout the entire Brooklyn Rapid Transit system.

| | **9980** | **Treadwell** | | __/1905 |

This is a double truck 600 volt direct current dump car that was a former Brooklyn Heights Railroad car acquired circa 1947, it was used to switch the Thirty-Ninth Street Yard, retired 1955.

General Roster Notes and Comments

In addition to the above rolling stock, one former box motor; a former Staten Island Rapid Transit car sold to the New York City Transit Authority; and three wood boxcars from the Singer Company at Elizabeth, New Jersey appeared to be the property of the South Brooklyn Railway. All of these cars were used as sheds during various periods of the road's history. There is one locomotive not shown in the above roster, this is a New York City Transit Authority Whitcomb diesel electric locomotive which carried the number 9. Similar to the South Brooklyn's number 8 and 9, it was never on the roster of the South Brooklyn Railway.

Davidson's Pipe Yard was the site of the locomotive terminal for the South Brooklyn Railroad during the latter part of the era of locomotives 12 and 13; it was often mistakenly reported in the rail fan press that these two locomotives had been sold to Davidson's.

- * * * -

A FIRST CLASS INTERURBAN ON THE SOUTH BROOKLYN RAILWAY

A predecessor of the Chicago, North Shore and Milwaukee Railroad opened an interurban railway between Milwaukee, Wisconsin and Evanston, Illinois as of October 31, 1908. Service between Evanston and the Loop in Chicago traveled over the lines of the Chicago Elevated. Besides a regular service of local trains the 'North Shore Line' also began the operation of express interurban trains between the two cities. The North Shore was in direct competition with two steam railroads with this service so, to keep pace with the Pullman cars of the Chicago Northwestern and the Milwaukee Road it began to offer upgraded or first class service, initially with a group of three wooden parlor buffet cars in 1909. Eventually the wood cars were set aside in favor of steel cars; eventually a fleet of seventeen first class cars were acquired of which five were non motorized parlor observation cars, generally considered some of the most luxurious interurban cars ever built. Cars 410 to 411 were built in 1923 by the Cincinnati Car Company, cars 412 to 413 in 1924 also by Cincinnati, and the last, the 420 by the Pullman Company in 1928. With the onset of World War II all five of these cars were rebuilt as double ended motorized high capacity coaches and were used in suburban locals out of Chicago to Mundelein.

As we said, parlor observation car 411 was built by the Cincinnati Car Company in 1923; it was converted to a high capacity motorized coach with a control position at each end as of February 25, 1943. The controls and electrical gear for the conversion came from retired box motors. It should be noted that the coach seats did not line up with the windows, a condition that continued to bedevil its riders until the North Shore quit running at 2:54 AM on January 20, 1963. After closure the car was sold to a railfan named Everett White, a New York City based trolley enthusiast who was acquiring a fleet of cars for his nascent Trolley Museum of New York which he had founded in 1955. The 411 was moved to Brooklyn and stored at the Coney Island Shops of the New York City Transit Authority joining the former Brooklyn and Queens Transit Presidential Conference Committee car 1000, the Brooklyn and Queens Transit Peter Witt car 8361, a Philadelphia 'Hog Island' car that had once been Ocean Electric 41, and Queensborough Bridge Railway 601. A former Staten Island Midland Railway carbody was located in Staten Island but it was determined that this car was too far gone for restoration.

The Trolley Museum of New York would eventually find a home in Kingston, New York.

Sold to a private owner, the former Chicago, North Shore and Milwaukee Railroad 411 departs the Coney Island Shops via the South Brooklyn Railway on June 21, 1973. The former observation car was being moved to the East Troy Railroad in Wisconsin for continued storage; it eventually was moved to the Escanaba and Lake Superior Railroad. The image on the left was taken by Doug Grotjahn and was provided by Joseph Torregrose. The image on the right was taken by the late Gerald Landau and was provided by John Scala. That sedan in the right image was acting as an end of train escort.

- * * * -

THE SHORTLINE RAILROADS OF LONG ISLAND

Finis

- * * * -

EPILOGUE

Of the mainline railroad freight delivery stations covered in this volume, all were shut down in the period covered by this material. The demise of the Jay Street Connecting Railway; the Degnon Terminal area of the Long Island Rail Road; and the Delaware, Lackawanna and Western Railroad facilities have already been covered. The South Brooklyn Railway, as documented, has had its line severely curtailed to but a few blocks in Brooklyn east of the Bush Terminal area.

As for the Brooklyn Eastern District Terminal, the New York Dock Railway, and the Bush Terminal Railroad, the story, while told in the preceding chapters needs a few more lines

Brooklyn Eastern District Terminal

The New York Dock Company had purchased all of the stock of the Brooklyn Eastern District Terminal in 1973 which insured the continuation of service to Pigeon Street in Long Island City; the North 10th Street complex in Williamsburg, and the contract switching service to the former Brooklyn Navy Yard. The Pigeon Street operation would cease on Conrail Day in 1976. Service to the North 10th Street area would be discontinued as of August 17, 1983. The last carloads into the former Brooklyn Navy Yard, now a New York City Industrial Park appear to have been moved sometime during 1985.

Bush Terminal Railroad

On December 31, 1971 the Bush Terminal Railroad was officially abandoned although some foreign line cars were handled on January 1, 1972. The Interstate Commerce Commission issued a directed service order to the New York Dock Railway in April 1972 and rail service resumed in the Bush Terminal area under the New York Dock Railway; eventually the New York Dock Railway would merge the rail assets of the Bush Terminal into its corporation during 1975.

New York Dock Railway

Traditionally this line operated three separate facilities, Atlantic Terminal, Baltic Terminal, and Fulton Terminal. The Baltic terminal was closed down during the early 1960's. As mentioned above, the New York Dock Railway acquired stock control of the Brooklyn Eastern District Terminal during 1973 but no merger of the two rail companies took place. Earlier, in April 1972 the New York Dock Railway had begun the operation of the former Bush Terminal Railway properties as a result of an Interstate Commerce Commission directed service order; the rail assets of Bush Terminal would be merged into the New York Dock Railway during 1975. Despite the positive outlook of the New York Dock Railway in the early 1970's, it had turned bleak by the early 1980's. The Fulton Terminal, the Atlantic Terminal, and the Brooklyn Eastern District Terminal were shut down on August 17, 1983; while this is where this volume's coverage halts; that is not where this story ends.

- * * * -

The New York Cross Harbor Railroad took over the operation of the former properties of the New York Dock Railway, the Bush Terminal Railroad, and the Brooklyn Eastern District Terminal as of August 17, 1983. The new operator was based in the former Bush Terminal yard and continued to serve the New York Dock's Atlantic Terminal and the contract switching duties of the Brooklyn Eastern District Terminal at the former Brooklyn Navy Yard. Locomotives from all three predecessor operators passed to the New York Cross Harbor but only three Alco S-1's from the Brooklyn Eastern District Terminal and two Electromotive Division NW-2's from the New York Dock Railway were put into use by the new line. The other three Alco S-1's from the Brooklyn Eastern District Terminal, the five General Electric center cabs from the New York Dock Railway; and the two Alco RS-2's that the New York Dock Railway had purchased to operate the former Bush Terminal were of no use to the

Cross Harbor. These ten locomotives were all loaded on a carfloat which was anchored at the former New York Dock Company's Fulton Terminal. This 'roster on the raft'[1] stayed there for three years in the view of passing motorists, only one of the locomotives stored there escaped a 1986 scrapping, and that one also eventually had its own meeting with the torch.

The Cross Harbor had intentions of improving connections with New Jersey and acquired the rights to use a portion of the old Long Island Rail Road Bay Ridge yard; the Port Authority funded the construction of two new float bridges at this site. These float bridges were never used. Service to both the Atlantic Terminal and the Brooklyn Navy Yard ceased between 1985 and 1992; Fulton Terminal was never used for anything but locomotive storage. The Brooklyn Eastern District's North 10th Street Complex was similarly never restored to operation. The New York and Cross Harbor did acquire a portion of the former Pennsylvania Railroad's Greenville yard and float bridges in Jersey City, New Jersey; initially a former Brooklyn Eastern District Terminal locomotive would be stationed there. The northern portion of the Bush Terminal between the main yard and the interchange with the South Brooklyn Railway apparently ceased being utilized in the mid to late 1990's.

The Cross Harbor eventually replaced their inherited fleet with additional used Electromotive Division switch locomotives. There was even a brief flirtation with the idea of using a trio of Alco Century 424's as mothers to a fleet of slugs created from retired Brooklyn Eastern District Terminal Alco S-1's; but this did not come to fruition. Even a used General Electric U23B mainline diesel locomotive was on the roster for about five years.

The New York Cross Harbor Railroad was purchased during 2006 by a new company named Mid Atlantic New England Rail, LLC based in West Seneca, New York who renamed it New York New Jersey Rail. During November 2008 New York New Jersey Rail was sold to the Port Authority of New York and New Jersey; the Greenville yard property would be acquired by the Port Authority after November 2011. The Port Authority has committed money to rebuilding a portion of the former Bush Terminal rail property in Brooklyn and to invest significant sums in the Greenville yard property. Construction of a connecting track to the South Brooklyn Railway is ongoing; part of a project identified as the South Brooklyn Marine Rail Terminal. This will bear watching.

- * * * -

---

[1] An image of this 'roster on the raft' taken by Jeff Erlitz on September 18, 1983 can be found on the back cover of this volume.

BIBLIOGRAPHY

Archer, Robert F.: **A HISTORY OF THE LEHIGH VALLEY RAILROAD – The Route of the Black Diamond**; Howell-North Books; Berkeley, California; Second Printing, 1978.

Benedict, Roy G. (editor): **BULLETIN 106 OF THE CENTRAL ELECTRIC RAILFANS' ASSOCIATION – Interurban to Milwaukee**; Central Electric Railfans' Association; Chicago, Illinois; Second Edition, 1974.

Benedict, Roy G. (editor): **BULLETIN 107 OF THE CENTRAL ELECTRIC RAILFANS' ASSOCIATION – Route of the Electroliners**; Central Electric Railfans' Association; Chicago, Illinois; Second Edition, 1975.

Burgess, George H.; and Kennedy, Miles C.: **CENTENNIAL HISTORY OF THE PENNSYLVANIA RAILROAD COMPANY – 1846-1946**; Pennsylvania Railroad; Philadelphia, Pennsylvania; 1949.

Carlson, Norman: **BULLETIN 114 OF THE CENTRAL ELECTRIC RAILFANS' ASSOCIATION – Iowa Trolleys**; Central Electric Railfans' Association; Chicago, Illinois; 1975.

Claflin, Jim; Dawson, Dick; Dover, Dan; Douglas, Ken; and Volkmer, Bill: 'Roster of Penn Central + NYC + PRR + NH' Part II' in **Extra 2200 South** (periodical); Volume 7, Number 11, June 1969; Dover Publications; Cincinnati, Ohio, 1969.

Copeland, Allan; and Dover, Dan: 'GE 44 Tonners' in **Extra 2200 South** (periodical), Issues 51 and 52, March-April 1975 and May-June 1975; Dover Publications; Cincinnati, Ohio, 1975.

Corley, Raymond R. and Hamley, David H.: 'How It All Began', **Trains** (periodical) Volume 34, Numbers 1, 2, and 3, November 1973, December 1973, and January 1974; Kalmbach Publications; Milwaukee, Wisconsin, 1973.

Cox, Harold E.: **THE BIRNEY CAR**: Harold E. Cox: Forty-Fort, Pennsylvania; Undated.

Cunningham, Joseph; and DeHart, Leonard: **HISTORY OF THE NEW YORK CITY SUBWAY SYSTEM, PART II – Rapid Transit in Brooklyn**; Joseph Cunningham; and Leonard DeHart; Brooklyn, New York; 1977.

Dover Dan; Goldsmith, Harold; Hamley, Dave; Kahn, Elliot; and Votava, George: 'Old Rare or Obscure (Especially Shortlines and Industrials)' in **Extra 2200 South** (periodical) Issue 60, April-May-June 1977; Dover Publications; Cincinnati, Ohio, 1977.

Dover, Dan: 'Alco HH Roster' in **Extra 2200 South** (periodical); Issue 35, July-August 1972; Dover Publications; Cincinnati, Ohio, 1972.

Edson, William D. **KEYSTONE STEAM AND ELECTRIC – Record of Steam and Electric Locomotives built for the Pennsylvania Railroad since 1906**; Wayner Publications; New York, New York; 1974.

Emery, Robert 'Bob': **BRT (BMT LINES) ELEVATED LINES – SUBWAY LINES**; unpublished manuscript notes.

Emery, Robert 'Bob': **BRT STREET CAR LINES**; unpublished manuscript notebook; undated

Extra 2200 South (periodical): various news articles and features; Dover Publications, Cincinnati, Ohio.

Foster, George H.; and Ziel, Ron: **STEEL RAILS TO THE SUNRISE**; Duel, Sloan and Pearce; New York, New York; 1965.

Foster, George H.; and Ziel, Ron: **STEEL RAILS TO THE SUNRISE**; Hawthorn Books Incorporated; New York, New York; Undated.

Goldstein, Philip M.: website found at http://members.trainweb.com/bedt/IndustrialLocos.html

Hamley, David H.: 'Ingersoll-Rand: Catalyst of Dieselization' in **Trains** (periodical), Volume 31, Number 2, December 1970; Kalmbach Publications; Milwaukee, Wisconsin, 1970.

Johnson, Gus: **F.D.N.Y. – The Fire Buff's Handbook of the New York Fire Department 1900-1975**; Western Island Books; Boston, Massachusetts, 1977.

Kahn, Alan Paul; and May, Jack: **TRACKS OF NEW YORK – Volume 2 - Brooklyn Elevated Railroads - 1910**; Electric Railroaders' Association; New York, New York; 1975.

Linder, Bernard: 'Bush Terminal Railroad Company' in **New York Division ERA Bulletin** (periodical) for December 1984; New York Division of the Electric Railfans Association; New York, New York, 1984

Long Island Rail Road Public Relations Department (Paul A. Blauvelt, Editor): **Long Island Railroader** (periodical) for April 24, 1958, Volume 3, Number 9; Long Island Rail Road; Jamaica, New York, 1958

BIBLIOGRAPHY

Moody's Investor Services: **GUIDE TO INDUSTRIALS MANUAL FOR 1952** (annual); Moody's Investor Services; New York, New York, 1952

Moody's Investor Services: **GUIDE TO RAILWAYS AND TRANSPORTATION COMPANIES** (annual); Moody's Investor Services; New York, New York, various years.

Pennypacker, Bertram S.; and Staufer, Alvin F.: **PENNSY POWER II – Steam, Diesel, and Electric Locomotives of the Pennsylvania Railroad**; Alvin F. Staufer / Staufer Publishing Company; Medina, Ohio (but Unstated); 1968.

Pinkepanke, Jerry: **DIESEL SPOTTERS GUIDE**; Kalmbach Books, Milwaukee, Wisconsin, 1967.

Pinkepanke, Jerry: **THE SECOND DIESEL SPOTTERS GUIDE**; Kalmbach Books, Milwaukee, Wisconsin, 1973.

Prince, Richard E.: **NORFOLK AND WESTERN RAILWAY – Pocahontas Coal Carrier – Precision Transportation**; Richard E. Prince, Millard, Nebraska, 1980.

Roseman, Victor: 'By Carfloat to Brooklyn' in **Trains** (periodical) Volume 50, Number 3 January 1989; Kalmbach Publications; Milwaukee, Wisconsin, 1989.

Scala, John J.: **DIESELS OF THE SUNRISE TRAIL – Color Compendium of Long Island Rail Road Diesels, Electric Locomotives . . .** ; Weekend Chief Publishing Company; Mineola, New York; 1984.

Seyfried, Vincent F.: **THE LONG ISLAND RAIL ROAD - A COMPREHENSIVE HISTORY – Part 5 – The Bay Ridge and Manhattan Beach Divisions; L.I.R.R. operations on the Brighton and Culver Lines**; Vincent F. Seyfried; Garden City, New York; 1966.

Seyfried, Vincent F.: **THE LONG ISLAND RAIL ROAD - A COMPREHENSIVE HISTORY – Part 7 – The Age of Electrification**; Vincent F. Seyfried; Garden City, New York; 1984.

Swanberg, J.W.: **NEW HAVEN POWER - 1838-1968 – Steam, Diesel, Electric, MU's, Trolleys, Motor Cars, Buses, and Boats**; Alvin F. Staufer / Staufer Publishing Company; Medina, Ohio; 1988.

Taber, Thomas Townsend (deceased) and Taber, Thomas Townsend, III: **THE DELAWARE, LACKAWANNA & WESTERN IN THE TWENTIETH CENTURY – VOLUME I- History and Operation**; published by Thomas Townsend Taber III; Muncy, Pennsylvania, 1980.

Taber, Thomas Townsend (deceased) and Taber, Thomas Townsend, III: **THE DELAWARE, LACKAWANNA & WESTERN IN THE TWENTIETH CENTURY – VOLUME II – Equipment and Marine**; published by Thomas Townsend Taber III; Muncy, Pennsylvania, 1981.

Taber, Thomas Townsend (deceased): **THE DELAWARE, LACKAWANNA & WESTERN IN THE NINTEENTH CENTURY- The Road of Anthracite**; published by Thomas Townsend Taber III; Muncy, Pennsylvania, 1977.

The Shortline (periodical): various news articles and feature articles; McDonald Publishing, Pleasant Garden, North Carolina.

Wayner, Robert J. (editor): **ELECTRIC LOCOMOTIVE ROSTERS**; Robert J. Wayner Publications; New York, New York, 1965.

- * * * -

The
LONG ISLAND – SUNRISE TRAIL CHAPTER
of the
NATIONAL RAILWAY HISTORICAL SOCIETY

The Long Island – Sunrise Trail Chapter of the National Railway Historical Society is a non profit Internal Revenue Code section 501(c)(3) educational organization. The Chapter was founded in 1966 to serve the railroad history needs of the Long Island region. Membership in the Chapter is available to all interested in railroad history. For further information about membership and other publications available from the Chapter please address mail inquiries to the Long Island – Sunrise Trail Chapter, National Railway Historical Society; Post Office Box 507; Babylon, New York, 11702-0507. Additional information can also be found on the Chapter's website located at http://list-nrhs.org. E-Mail inquiries should be addressed to the Chapter at LISunriseTrail@yahoo.com.

- * * * -